Key Topics in Children's Emotional Development

||||||||||||||||||||||||||||||||||||
I0125271

Key Topics in Children's Emotional Development explores how children express, understand, and manage their emotions. From infancy to young adulthood, the book examines how young people develop feelings such as happiness, fear, anger, sadness, and empathy, while also addressing the challenges some face in managing these emotions. It introduces the foundational theories, methodologies, and historical context of emotional development, providing a comprehensive framework for understanding children's emotional growth.

The book delves into the development of key emotions and the pathways that may lead to clinically significant emotional problems, such as anxiety, phobias, depression, and conduct disorder. Organized to reflect the ages at which children begin to express different emotions, it pairs chapters on primary emotions with discussions of individual differences and related emotional disorders. Additionally, it explores contemporary issues affecting young people's emotional well-being, including loneliness, body image concerns, gender dysphoria, racism, political unrest, and climate change. The book highlights the latest prevention and intervention strategies, offering practical insights for addressing children's mental health challenges.

This book is an essential resource for students of developmental and abnormal psychology, as well as those studying educational, clinical, and forensic psychology. It will also appeal to postgraduate students pursuing professional qualifications in psychiatry, social work, paediatric nursing, teaching, and early childhood education.

Dale F. Hay is Professor Emerita in the School of Psychology at Cardiff University. She is Developmental Psychologist whose studies of children's development have been funded by the Medical Research Council, the Wellcome Trust, the Waterloo Foundation in the UK, and the National Science Foundation in the US. She has written an earlier textbook on emotional development, co-authored a book on statistics, and edited a number of books on topics in developmental psychology.

BPS Key Topics in Psychology

British Psychological Society

Routledge, in partnership with the British Psychological Society (BPS), is pleased to present *BPS Key Topics in Psychology*, a series of short introductory books that focus on a specific field within psychology. Each book is broken down into bitesize chunks to provide a helpful overview of core psychology topics, made clear by a five-part structure: foundations, theories, methodologies, impacts, and emerging areas. Written by active and experienced authors, these essential books encourage students to approach fundamental concepts with confidence and critical thinking.

Books may incorporate student-friendly pedagogies, including tools such as: feature boxes; key terms and definitions; and links to further reading online. Concise yet comprehensive, these books offer a simple and accessible overview of core psychology topics for students looking for a summary of key concepts in the topic, or those new to the area.

For more information about this series, please visit: www.routledge.com/BPS-Key-Topics-in-Psychology/book-series/BPSKTP

Key Topics in Children's Emotional Development

Dale F. Hay

Routledge
Taylor & Francis Group

LONDON AND NEW YORK

Designed cover image: Getty © Westend61

First published 2026
by Routledge
4 Park Square, Milton Park, Abingdon, Oxon OX14 4RN

and by Routledge
605 Third Avenue, New York, NY 10158

Routledge is an imprint of the Taylor & Francis Group, an informa business

British Library Cataloguing-in-Publication Data
A catalogue record for this book is available from the British Library

ISBN: 978-1-032-77571-5 (hbk)
ISBN: 978-1-032-77499-2 (pbk)
ISBN: 978-1-003-48379-3 (ebk)

DOI: 10.4324/9781003483793

Typeset in Galliard
By Deanta Global Publishing Services, Chennai, India

Access the Support Material: www.routledge.com/9781032774992

Contents

Chapter 1

Introduction

The Importance of Studying Children's Emotions

Our social lives are bound up with our own feelings as well as the positive and negative emotions of the people we know and spend time with. As soon as we're born, we express our immediate feelings: we cry. Our first cries probably reflect the pain we experienced during our journey down the birth canal and the strange sounds and bright light now in our ears and eyes.

We may feel even more uncomfortable as we are moved about, placed in our mothers' arms and then, for those of us who are born in hospitals, taken away to be checked over for potential medical problems. The medics may be listening to the acoustic properties of our cries, which can sometimes indicate underlying medical problems (e.g., Lawford, Sazon, Richard, Robb, & Bora, 2022). In various cultures, childbirth does not typically take place in hospital settings and infants are born at home; midwives and other health professionals may strive to provide what has been termed 'culturally competent care' (e.g., Withers, Kharazmi, & Lim, 2018). However, across the broad range of cultural contexts, infants express emotions and adults try to soothe their distress.

The Emergence of Different Emotions

Over the next days and weeks, as our senses develop further, we may begin to experience different emotions: interest in the sights and sounds in the outside world; pleasure when fed and cuddled; and distress when we are cold or wet or in pain. For example, when they are awake, newborn infants gaze at their mothers' faces; over the next few months, they begin to gaze for longer periods of time at other features of their surroundings (e.g., Messinger, Ekas, Ruvolo, & Fogel, 2012).

Long before we are able to use words or gestures to communicate with other people, the sound of our cries and our facial expressions of emotion are already setting up channels of communication with our caregivers, signalling what we need. Infants cry in different ways, depending

DOI: 10.4324/9781003483793-1

on the circumstances that are causing their distress, such as being hungry, feeling pain, and being born. Initial studies of infants' cries drew upon observers' perceptions of infants' different types of cries. In recent years, investigators have used new technologies beyond their personal ratings of infants' emotional expressions. They may also make use of computer analyses, in particular machine learning techniques, to analyse the fine-grained acoustic qualities of infants' cries (e.g., Ji, Mudiyanselenge, Gao, & Pan, 2021).

Emotional development is interactive. Over the next few months, as infants pay attention to the people, objects, and events in their surroundings, they begin to coordinate their actions with other people's actions and reactions. They become able to decode other people's cues and respond to their caregivers' expressions of emotion. Some developmental scientists have argued that even newborns are able to imitate other people's facial expressions of emotion; what is certainly true is that when young infants express their discomfort, their parents and other caregivers begin to learn how to comfort the distressed infants. These interactions reveal a dynamic process; the more distressed the infants are, the more likely the adults looking after them may become upset as well. However, when infants begin to smile and laugh, the adults who care for them may often smile and laugh as well. Infants begin to express different types of emotions, not just general distress, and by three to four months of age, they play smiling games, timing their smiles in coordination with their parents (Ruvolo, Messinger, & Movellan, 2015).

During the first year, infants begin to cry in different ways, and their parents and other caregivers learn how to distinguish fearful, angry, and frustrated cries. The adults may also be learning to regulate their own emotions in the face of their infants' emotional needs. As we shall see in later chapters, infants themselves are sensitive to and react in different ways to other infants' cries. We shall also see that parents' own emotional states will affect the quality of their interactions with their infants, which in turn influences the infants' emotions.

Key Features of Emotional Development

Parallel Processes in Development

Emotional development takes place in parallel with other developmental processes, such as learning to crawl and walk and eventually run, or learning how to communicate with other people, using both non-verbal gestures and words. Like other strands of human development, emotional development is dynamic and multi-faceted. Infants' early non-verbal expressions of emotion change and consolidate as they grow older and experience both pleasant and unpleasant events. Eventually, they will feel mixed emotions.

Dynamic Features of Emotional Development

Emotions are dynamic. Theorists of emotion have pointed out that emotions are not static conditions but rather processes that ebb and flow as we engage with the people and events in our worlds. As emotion theorists have explained:

> Emotions are not 'things,' they are processes and as such they are themselves change—the result in change between the environment and person; the emergent sum of multi-faceted change in mind, brain, and body; and the spark for subsequent change in the relation between person and environment as emotions motivate actions and reactions.
>
> (Hastings & Kahle, 2019)

Expressions of particular emotions may be the result of fleeting moods, or sudden reactions to surprise or threat, or enduring feelings that have grown and consolidated over time.

Neurobiological Underpinnings of Emotional Development

Emotional development is supported by other dimensions of children's biological development. Their growing abilities to express, perceive, and comprehend emotions are bound up with stressful experiences, hormonal influences, brain development, and cognitive attainments. For example, the hormonal changes that girls and boys experience during puberty affect their abilities to process other people's emotions (e.g., Vijakumar, Pfeifer, Flournoy, Hernandez, & Dapretto, 2019).

Understanding Other People's Emotions

Emotional development is not just about expressing our own feelings; even young infants learn to recognize the facial and vocal expressions of emotion shown by other people. Experimental studies of infants' attention to photographs and videos of adults' faces have shown that infants pay attention to the emotions being communicated by other people's facial expressions. In particular, by the midpoint of the first year, infants seem especially sensitive to adults' fearful expressions (Leppanen & Nelson, 2012). This may be the way we first identify sources of danger in our worlds. Infants are also sensitive to other infants' emotions, paying attention to other infants' crying and sometimes starting to cry themselves (e.g., Hay, Nash, & Pedersen, 1981).

Sensitivity and Insensitivity to Other People's Emotions

As children grow older, they draw on their understanding of themselves and others to be more sensitive—or in some cases less sensitive—to other people's feelings (e.g., Acland, Jambon, & Multi, 2021). Their own expressions of emotion become more complex and nuanced. Some children learn how to mask their own emotions. For example, in an experimental study where five- and seven-year-old children were given a disappointing gift (Davis, 1995), some children tried to disguise their disappointment; girls were somewhat more likely than boys to pretend to like their unwanted gift.

Understanding and Explaining Feelings of Ourselves and Others

Once they acquire language, children may try to explain how they feel. They also begin to understand how their expressions of emotions affect other people. In some circumstances, children may try their best to disguise their feelings, but their faces and voices are likely to reveal how they feel and what they need. In later childhood and adolescence, they may discover new ways to hide or disguise their feelings from other people. Their feelings may become more nuanced over time, influenced by the context in which they are growing up and the positive experiences as well as the stressors that are affecting their lives. Life events and social challenges may reduce happiness and provoke sadness and anger. Young people who are less aware and less likely to value their own emotions are more likely to experience anxiety and depression (Rieffe & De Rooij, 2012).

Emotions in the Social Context of Children's Lives

Emotional development is fundamentally social. Children not only develop the abilities to express their emotions but also to decode and respond to other people's emotional expressions. Even in the first year of life, infants not only cry but react to other infants' cries and adults' expressions of worry and sorrow. The expression of emotion can become contagious, as when one young child finds something funny and other children laugh as well. For example, children laugh harder at funny videos when they're watching with other children than when they're on their own (Addyman, Fogelquist, Levakova, & Rees, 2018). Eventually as children grow older and experience both pleasant and upsetting events, their expression of primary emotions explodes into more complex blends of feelings.

Aims of the Book

In writing this book, I had two aims. The first aim was to trace the development of the expression and regulation of different emotions over time, from infancy to young adulthood. Most primary emotions emerge in infancy and early childhood. Chapters that feature each of these primary emotions (fear, disgust, happiness, anger, empathy, and sadness) are presented in the order in which children begin to express them in infancy and early childhood.

My second aim was to emphasize that there are many individual differences in children's emotional development. Some children may struggle to contain their emotions and only gradually learn how to regulate their feelings; some children follow developmental pathways that take them toward clinically significant emotional problems. Precursors to emotional disorders such as anxiety or depression often emerge in early childhood and consolidate over middle childhood and adolescence.

To demonstrate how such emotional problems develop over childhood and adolescence, each chapter that describes the development of a particular emotion is followed by a chapter that focuses on a clinically defined emotional disorder related to that emotion. For example, the chapter on the development of fear is immediately followed by the chapter on clinically significant anxiety disorders, which may affect a proportion of children and adolescents. It is usual for children's development and their mental health problems to be taught separately in different modules. However, in this book, the emergence of emotional disorders is examined within a developmental framework.

Structure of the Book

The book begins by placing the study of emotional development in a historical and theoretical perspective. In Chapter 2, you will read about the long history of parents' and scholars' interest in children's feelings and trace the development of very different psychological theories of emotional development. In Chapter 3, you will learn about the various methods that developmental psychologists have devised to study children's emotional outbursts and their reactions to emotional challenges. This chapter will focus on the designs of different sorts of studies, both experimental and correlational, both cross-sectional and longitudinal. Some of the methods used in older studies might no longer seem quite ethical;

however, new technologies for assessing children's emotions have been developed in recent years. You will learn about a variety of studies conducted in different places in the world, focusing on different age groups and different circumstances in which children are growing up.

Chapter 4 provides information about the earliest expressions of emotion that infants show in their first months of life: crying, smiling, and laughing. These fundamental expressions of emotion allow infants to communicate their needs to their parents and other people who may be looking after them. Their facial expressions supplement their cries of distress and thus provide important cues for parents and other caregivers, enabling them to understand the infants' feelings, needs, and desires.

In Chapters 5–11, we shall trace the emergence, development, and growing understanding of the primary emotions in infancy and early childhood. In these chapters, we also draw attention to the emotional problems experienced by older children and adolescents. The chapters on the development of specific emotions—fear, disgust, anger, empathy, and sadness—are interwoven with chapters that discuss children's and adolescents' clinically significant emotional problems.

These paired chapters on basic emotions and associated emotional problems are set out roughly in the order in which each primary emotion emerges during the child's development. In Chapter 5, we trace the development of the primary emotions of fear and disgust from infancy to later childhood. Chapter 6 then focuses on individual differences in children's fearfulness; their later worries and phobias which are generated by both fear and disgust; and, in some cases, their experiences of clinically diagnosed panic attacks and anxiety disorders.

The next emotions to be discussed in Chapter 7 are frustration and anger, which emerge in infancy and early childhood. In this chapter, we examine those emotions as they are expressed in children's conflicts with parents, siblings, other caregivers, teachers, and peers. Anger is a basic emotion, and conflicts are frequent occurrences in social life, shown by most people starting in the first two years of life. However, despite anger being a primary emotion that we all feel in some circumstances, there are clear individual differences in infants' and young children's angry feelings. Individual children who are prone to anger have been variously referred to as irritable, having difficult temperaments, and showing angry aggressiveness.

In Chapter 8, we examine these individual differences in anger and conflict in more detail and trace how some young children's outbursts of anger and irritability are first steps on a pathway toward the clinical diagnosis of a behavioural problem, oppositional defiant disorder (ODD). Next, in Chapter 9, we continue to focus on the emotional underpinnings of a clinically defined behavioural disorder, in this case, conduct disorder (CD). Conduct disorder is often associated with physical aggression, but it is also measured by other behaviours, including cruelty and destructiveness. Children and adolescents who are diagnosed with conduct disorder often show low levels of the positive emotion of empathy.

Chapter 9 begins with a description of the early development of empathy for other people's emotions, starting with infants' well-documented tendencies to cry when other infants cry. This emotional response to other infants' cries could possibly be explained as simply a negative reaction to an annoying sound; however, this kind of contagious crying is soon followed by very young children's attempts to comfort other people who are in distress. These early attempts to bring comfort to others are a clear sign of early empathy.

Empathy is sometimes seen as a moral emotion. In the preschool years, children are also beginning to develop two other moral emotions: feelings of shame and guilt. In Chapter 9, we examine how children and adolescents who show little empathy, shame, or guilt often follow a path toward conduct disorder.

Next, in Chapter 10, we draw attention to another primary emotion that is already evident in very early childhood: sadness. Feelings of sadness are triggered by particular events that evoke disappointment and loss. In this chapter, we examine studies of different types of losses that provoke children's sadness. These losses may be quite temporary (such as being briefly separated from a parent or feeling homesick while attending a summer camp) or permanent (moving house or changing schools). Some losses are permanent and lead to deep sadness. Even young children experience bereavements when pets, grandparents, or parents die.

Such major losses and other troubles in their lives may affect children and adolescents so strongly that they experience clinical depression. In Chapter 11, we note that clinicians finally acknowledged that young people experience depression, and that even quite young children can experience clinically defined depression. The symptoms that define depressive disorders in adults are also observed in children and adolescents. Thus, in Chapter 11, we focus on the genetic risk factors, life events and other upsetting circumstances in the family, school, and the situations in which children live that put them at elevated risk for depressive disorders and bipolar illness.

In the final two chapters, we focus on the broader contexts of children's emotional development and risk for emotional problems and clinical disorders. In Chapter 12, we shall examine whether children's environments promote healthy emotional development, the risks for emotional problems that endure at present, and the ongoing efforts in the UK to promote positive emotions and reduce children's and adolescents' risks for serious emotional problems.

Finally, in Chapter 13, I have tried to highlight the state of our current knowledge and the need for further exploration of children's emotional lives. In this final chapter, I have suggested several important topics in the domain of young people's emotions that have not yet been explored in sufficient depth and should be investigated more deeply. It is my hope that some of you who are reading this book will become the future investigators and clinicians who will teach us even more about children's and adolescents' emotional development.

References

Acland, E. L., Jambon, M., & Malti, T. (2021). Children's emotion recognition and aggression: A multi-cohort longitudinal study. *Aggressive Behaviour*, *47*, 646–658.

Addyman, C., Fogelquist, C., Levakova, L., & Rees, S. (2018). Social facilitation of laughter and smiles in preschool children. *Frontiers in Psychology*, *9*, 1048.

Davis, T. L. (1995). Gender differences in masking negative emotions: Ability or motivation? *Developmental Psychology*, *31*, 660–667.

Hastings, P. D., & Kahle, S. (2019). Get bent into shape: The non-linear, multi-system, contextually-embedded psychophysiology of emotional development. In V. LoBue, K. Pérez-Edgar, & K. A. Buss (Eds.), *Handbook of emotional development*. Cham: Springer.

Hay, D. F., Nash, A., & Pedersen, J. (1981). Responses of six-month-olds to the distress of their peers. *Child Development*, *52*, 1071–1076.

Ji, C., Mudiyanselage, T. B., Gao, Y., & Pan, Y. (2021). A review of infant cry analysis and classification. *EURASIP Journal on Audio, Speech, and Music Processing*, *2021*, Article 8.

Lawford, H. L. S., Sazon, H., Richard, C., Robb, M. P., & Bora, S. (2022). Acoustic cry characteristics of infants as a marker of neurological dysfunction: A systematic review and meta-analysis. *Pediatric Neurology*, *129*, 72–79.

Leppanen, J. M., & Nelson, C. A. (2012). Early development of fear processing. *Current Directions in Psychological Science*, *21*, 200–204.

Messinger, D. S., Ekas, N. V., Ruvolo, P., & Fogel, A. D. (2012). 'Are you interested, baby?' Young infants exhibit stable patterns of attention during interaction. *Infancy*, *17*, 233–244.

Rieffe, C., & de Rooij, M. (2012). The longitudinal relationship between emotion Awareness and internalising symptoms during late childhood. *European Child and Adolescent Psychiatry*, *21*, 349–356.

Ruvolo, P., Messinger, D., & Movellan, J. (2015). Infants time their smiles to make their moms smile. *PLoS One*, *10*, e0136492.

Vijakumar, N., Pfeifer, J. H., Flournoy, J. C., Hernandez, L. M., & Dapretto, M. (2019). Affective reactivity during adolescence: Associations with age, puberty, and testosterone. *Cortex*, *117*, 336–350.

Withers, M., Kharazmi, N., & Lim, E. (2018). Traditional beliefs and practices in pregnancy, childbirth and postpartum: A review of the evidence from Asian countries. *Midwifery*, *56*, 158–170.

Key Foundations, Theories, and Methodologies

At the end of Section 1, you will have:

- Learned about the importance of studying emotional development from infancy to young adulthood.
- Understood the structure of this book, which will teach you about children's expression of the ways they feel, their understanding of their own and other people's emotions, and their vulnerability to various emotional problems.
- Learned about the history of the study of children's emotions over the last three centuries, beginning with scientists' observations of their own children and leading up to the key issues in contemporary developmental science.
- Become familiar with the most common research designs and methods used to study emotional development and emotional problems.

DOI: 10.4324/9781003483793-2

Chapter 2

The Study of Children's Emotional Development

The high rates and continuing rise of emotional problems in childhood and adolescence are a matter of great concern to parents, teachers, clinicians, policymakers and, most importantly, the distressed children and teenagers themselves. Some of the increase in young people's anxiety and depression can be attributed to family crises, economic pressures, exposure to violence and warfare, and the experience of isolation in response to the global pandemic. However, it is important to take a broader perspective and trace general developmental trends in emotional expression and emotional understanding from infancy to young adulthood. It is also important to study children's positive emotional experiences as well as their sadness, anger, and fearfulness. In doing so, we draw upon a longstanding tradition of adults' fascination with children's emotions and the importance of studies of emotional development within the history of psychology.

Historical Interest in Parents' and Children's Emotions

Ancient Texts

Ever since ancient times, children's feelings, as well as parents' conflicted feelings about their children, have drawn the attention of storytellers, artists, and writers. Some of our earliest texts tell stories about parents killing their children as a religious sacrifice or a political necessity. For example, in the Old Testament of the Bible, the patriarch Abraham being ordered by his God to kill his young son Isaac. In the modern translations of this Bible story, God relents, and Isaac lives. However, one scholar has argued that in the earliest Hebrew texts, God did not change his mind and Abraham killed his son, as God had instructed.

The death of a politically important child also appears in the stories told by the ancient Greeks. In the *Iliad*, which tells the story of the war between Greece and Troy, the Trojan king Hector is defeated, and his

DOI: 10.4324/9781003483793-3

son Astyanax is killed by the Greek victor, Odysseus. However, prior to the defeat of Troy, King Hector meets with his wife and son. Astyanax does not recognize his father, who is wearing an unfamiliar plumed helmet, and begins to cry. This ancient account of a young child's fearful reaction to such a strange situation predates our later understanding of children's reactions to strangers and the disruption of the relationship between parents and children.

Victorian Novels about Difficult Childhoods

In the 18th and 19th centuries, readers became increasingly fascinated by coming-of-age stories, often tales of success in adulthood after many trials and tribulations in childhood and mishaps or bad choices in adolescence. For example, in her novel *Jane Eyre*, Charlotte Bronte provided detailed scenes of a lonely, rejected child's struggles to control her own rage and frustration, to be seen and not heard by whatever adults were meant to be looking after her. Her contemporaries such as Charles Dickens and Elizabeth Gaskell wrote realistic accounts of children's grief at the deaths of parents or siblings. In such novels, such authors drew attention to children's depth of emotion and lack of protection from adults who should be caring for them. While some of these fictional children were rescued by kind adults or unknown benefactors, many of the adult characters showed little or no understanding of the depth of children's feelings and offered no emotional support. Such stories drew on adult readers' own emotions and helped draw attention to the desperate circumstances in which many children were living. However, the child protagonists often had to learn how to control their negative emotions if they were to take up a comfortable place in their societies. In real life, as opposed to novels, children who'd experienced deprivation and violence from others would not necessarily be able to learn how to manage their own emotions or deal with the negative emotions of others.

The depiction of child characters in Victorian novels seems to have produced a kind of empathy for children's problems in the adults who read the books. This drew attention to the difficult lives of impoverished and ill children that may have had an influence on the establishment of child-centred charitable foundations in 19th-century Britain.

Early Scientific Studies of Children's Emotional Development

Baby Biographies

Individual children's emotional experiences have been recorded by their parents and other people at least since the 18th century. Information about infants' emotions can be found in the 'baby biographies' recorded by parents who often were philosophers or scientists who were interested in the nature of human nature (e.g., Tiedemann, 1787, tr. Murchison & Langer, 1927), who recorded the everyday activities of their children. Although these reports often focused on motor, perceptual, and verbal development, the baby biographers also paid some attention to children's emotions (Darwin, 1887).

Baby Biographies

Detailed observations of infants and young children written by parents and other relatives. Samuel Coleridge, Charles Darwin, Friedrich Tiedemann, amongst other scholars and scientists, wrote baby biographies in the 18th and 19th centuries that recorded infants' emotions and skills which were later studied in larger samples.

For example, in the 19th century, the naturalist and evolutionary theorist Charles Darwin was acutely interested in the ways in which humans and other animals expressed their emotions. He began this line of work by writing a baby biography, keeping a diary in which he recorded the behaviour of his infant son William Erasmus, informally known as Doddy. Darwin believed that the behaviours shown by very young children were likely to be instinctual, provided in their evolutionary toolkits at birth rather than being taught or learned from their later experiences.

Darwin continued to record detailed observations of William's development for nearly five years. He reported that William was frowning by five days of age and moving his mouth into something like a smile at five weeks, although Darwin did not believe this meant that his infant son was truly experiencing happiness. Rather, he saw William's movement of his lips into a configuration that resembled a smile was exploration of his motor capabilities, not a communication of happiness. As William grew older, Darwin recorded some of his son's signs of pain or distress:

'When nine weeks & three days old—whilst lying on his back cooing & kicking very happily.—I happened to sneezed—which made it start, frown, look frightened & cry rather badly—For an hour afterwards, every noise made him start,—he was nervous.—I think he certainly has an undefined instinctive 7 fears—for instance when stripped naked—I think also when passing under dark doorway.— When hurt, & when first waking & stretching the blood rushes into his face.—After the above violent crying fit, his eyes were suffused, with tears.']

Some years after Darwin's observations of his son, several psychologists proposed that infants had 'primitive instincts' that emerged over the early months of life. For example, Ribot (1903) suggested that fear, which he considered to be a 'defensive' emotion, emerged prior to anger, which he considered an 'offensive' emotion, and 'affection' for other people, which led to later social and moral emotions.

Darwin's careful observations of his infant's emotional life, as well as the observations recorded by other 'baby biographers,' were foundational for a broader tradition of using direct observations in naturalistic settings when studying emotional development. However, later in the next century, more experimental methods began to be deployed in the study of children's emotions.

Early Twentieth Century Experiments

Darwin's observations had been made in the context of his theory of human evolution; he was striving to record human infants' natural expressions of emotion that would have emerged in the course of evolution. In the perspective of his own theory of evolution, Darwin would have assumed his son's emotional expressions as having been selected for in the course of human evolution (Watson & Raynor, 1920).

However, in the early twentieth century, psychologists' studies of children's emotions were not exclusively descriptive. Rather, they used experimental paradigms to study children's reactions to experiences that might provoke strong emotion. These early experimental psychologists were seeking evidence for the role of learning processes as well as instinctual reactions in infants' emotional development.

The experimental procedures that these experimental psychologists conducted were not always pleasant. At that point in time, psychology was defining itself as a rigorous, experimental science, and so a strict methodology was used in their studies of children's emotional learning. Some of the classic studied conducted in that period are now seen as ethically questionable experiments on young children's reactions to potentially frightening things. For example, in 1919, the learning theorists Watson and Rayner conditioned a young child to feel fear.

Watson and Raynor proposed that children would express three fundamental emotions that had evolved over time and were genetically based: fear, rage, and love. However, they hypothesized that the expressions of those emotions would also be influenced by their experiences. To test this hypothesis, they focused on the emotion of fear and tested for an infant's fearfulness in response to particular experiences and physical objects. They studied a nine-month-old infant whose mother was a wet nurse at a hospital (i.e., a woman who'd recently given birth to her own infant, who was referred to as Albert B, and was breastfeeding other infants). The authors, who described Albert as generally 'stolid and emotional,' tried to frighten him with 'a white rat, a dog, a monkey, masks with and without hair, cotton wool, burning newspapers' (p. 2); Albert showed no signs of fear of any of these animals and things. What did appear to upset him was a loud noise made by striking a steel bar behind his head. The experimenters then proceeded to teach him how to be frightened by other things, for example, showing Albert the white rat while making the loud noise behind his head. Eventually, Albert began to cry when he saw the white rat, even without hearing the loud noise. Subsequently, they taught him to be afraid of a rabbit and a dog.

Watson and Rayner's repeated attempts to teach an infant to be frightened of particular things would never be deemed ethical today. More recent studies of children's emotions have sought evidence for individual differences in children's emotional reactions to challenging situations, either directly observed or reported by parents and other people who know the children well. In these studies, however, unlike some of the earlier baby biographies, there is generally more emphasis on the things that make children frightened or sad than on the things that make children feel happy.

Key Theories of Emotional Development

In the 20th and 21st centuries, children's emotions have been studied in the context of several different theories—for example, ethological theory, which focused on innate forms of emotional expression in humans and other species; social learning theories, which examined children's emotions in terms of earlier rewards, punishments, and parents' own modelling of emotional expressions; and psychoanalytic theories, which called attention to children's early experiences with their parents. Psychoanalytic theory and ethology were particularly influential in the development of John Bowlby and Mary Ainsworth's attachment theory, a theory that remains important for the study of emotional development today. However, in the 21st century, neurobiological theories have also become important for the study of emotional development.

Attachment Theory

A theory of the development of the emotional relationship between a child and his or her caregiver, most often the parent A theory of the development of the emotional relationship between a child and his or her caregiver, most often the parent, developed originally by John Bowlby and Mary Ainsworth in the mid-20th century.

Evolutionary Theory and Ethology

In the late 19th century, as Darwin's theory of evolution became more broadly accepted, some scientists became interested in the evolutionary

Ethology

The study of animal behaviour in naturalistic settings, as opposed to experimental laboratories, with particular attention to species characteristics that have emerged in the course of evolution. In the 20th century, ethological theorists such as Konrad Lorenz and Niko Tinbergen identified species-specific behaviours in birds and mammals.

roots of behaviour shown in different species. They assumed that the processes of natural selection might influence the characteristic behaviour of members of a species, not just their appearance and perceptual abilities. This interest in behavioural observations of various species was consolidated in the 20th century and given the name *ethology*, a term derived from ancient Greek that means the study of character. An underlying assumption was that different species had evolved to adapt to their environments by behaving in distinct ways.

Ethology was primarily an observational science, where members of a given species were observed behaving freely in their natural environments, not in structured laboratory tasks. Ethologists assumed that the various things birds and mammals did in their natural environments were instinctual, behaviours that had evolved over the course of evolution.

Although ethologists were primarily focused on birds' and mammals' observable behaviour, not inner emotions, they did record observations of cases where the animals they were observing expressed specific emotions. For example, when a parent or companion died, mammals express grief in species-typical ways (Bekoff, 2005). In her long-term observations of a troop of chimpanzees, Jane Goodall (1990) described the extreme reactions of one chimpanzee to his mother's death, becoming lethargic, refusing food, and eventually falling ill and dying himself. These emotional reactions are not only seen in primates. Displays of emotional attachments and grief have also been observed in African elephants (Moss, 2000). In reviewing the ethological literature on emotions, Bekoff notes that some scientists disagree with the premise that animals' emotions are truly equivalent to humans' inner experiences when they express sadness, joy, anger, and so on. However, ethologists' observations of different species clearly demonstrate the expression of strong emotions in certain situations by non-human primates.

Later in the 20th century, some ethologists began to apply similar observational methods to the study of human interaction, as shown in childhood as well as adulthood (e.g., Blurton Jones, 1972; Eibl-Eibesfeldt, 1979). The human ethologists paid attention to characteristic ways of showing emotion, including facial expressions such as smiling or frowning and the tone of voice. Their attention to facial expressions and other emotional signals has influenced subsequent developmental research.

The ethologists' research also drew attention to the often unspoken rules about communicating one's feelings to others. The cultural norms that govern emotional expression are referred to as display rules (Ekman & Friesen, 1969). Young children in different cultures learn when and under what circumstances it is appropriate to express particular emotions (e.g., Cole, 1986). Display rules might be different for different people, depending on age, gender, and social norms.

Psychoanalytic Theories

Around the turn of the 20th century, another set of theories focused on infants' and children's inner experiences, not just their overt expressions of emotion. Sigmund Freud's psychoanalytic theory (Freud, 1920) drew attention to the importance of infants' emotional experiences with their mothers in the earliest years of life. One of the most important facets of psychoanalytic theory was the claim that children's emotions were already present at birth. For example, the psychoanalyst Susan Isaacs claimed that in early infancy 'knowledge is

Psychoanalytic Theory

A set of theories of human development and mental health that focuses on the long-term effects of infants' early experiences with their parents, beginning with the work of Sigmund Freud in the 19th century. Later psychoanalytic theorists included Alfred Adler and Melanie Klein, whose work also influenced clinical practice.

lacking, understanding has not yet begun, but wants and wishes, fears and angers, love and hate are there from the beginning' (Isaacs, 1968, cited in Jersild, 1946). In other words, in psychoanalytic thought, an infant's inner life was emotional, and the emotions felt were equivalent to those felt by older children and adults. Indeed, some psychoanalytic theorists such as Melanie Klein (1952) claimed that the emotions felt by infants as they were fed and cared for by their mothers were 'an essential part of a child's sexuality' (p. 31, quoted in Jersild, 1946).

The psychoanalytic focus on the importance of the relationship between a mother and infant has contributed to attachment theory, developed by John Bowlby and Mary Ainsworth in the 1960s (Ainsworth, 1969, 1985; Bowlby, 1969), which remains a very important theory of emotional development in this century. As we shall see in later chapters, attachment theory synthesizes some psychoanalytic perspectives with ethological approaches to parent-offspring relationships and some features of cognitive psychology. Subsequent developments in attachment theory have integrated Bowlby and Ainsworth's theory with other accounts of the gradual development of different emotions such as Katharine Bridges' differentiation theory (Bridges, 1932). Drawing upon various broader accounts of the roles of dynamic and organizational factors in children's emotional development, Alan Sroufe has noted that the different primary emotions do not all develop at the same rate and that the study of emotional development must be integrated with other cognitive and social theories (Sroufe, 1995). Attachment theory draws attention to individual differences in attachment styles (Ainsworth, Blehar, Waters, & Wall, 2015).

Learning Theories

The naturalistic observations recorded by ethologists stand in contrast to the experiments on animal learning conducted by psychologists in the mid-20th century, who developed several different research paradigms, such as classical conditioning (Pavlov, 1927), operant conditioning (Skinner, 1938), and observational learning (Bandura & Walters, 1963). Classical conditioning theories focus on associations between an unconditioned stimulus—an event that immediately evokes an emotional or behavioural reaction, such as crying out after experiencing a deafening sound or an electric shock—and a conditioned stimulus, such as the sound of a bell, which does not in itself have the power to frighten a person but becomes associated with the frightening event. For example, fearful responses such as sweating or a rapid heart rate can be conditioned to become associated with arbitrary stimuli such as a piece of music (e.g., Lindquist, 2020). In contrast, in operant conditioning, children learn to do things that are rewarded or punished, respectively. Many studies of operant conditioning focus on overt actions, rather than emotional expressions, and less is known about the influence of rewards or punishment on children's internal feelings.

Observational learning, such as watching an adult who is expressing a great deal of anger, can influence children's own emotional expression. For example, a child who observes another child's temper tantrum may copy some of the elements of the tantrum. However, it is not always clear whether the child who observes the tantrum is

Social Learning Theory

A developmental theory that emerged from behaviourist learning theories, which focuses on children's learning behaviours from other people, through processes of rewards and punishment and the imitation of role models. Social learning theorists such as Albert Bandura, Robert Cairns, and Gerald Patterson have often focused on children's socialization into the norms of their societies and also their imitation of undesirable behaviours.

experiencing the same feelings, as opposed to copying an interesting set of overt actions.

Dynamic Systems Theories

Whereas other theories focus on an adult or child's expression of emotion as an individual act, dynamic systems theorists consider emotions in a broader context: 'The features we emphasize are the following: (1) emotions are relational, not individual; (2) emotions are self-organizing systems, not generated outputs; and (3) emotions are processes of change, not states' (Fogel et al., 1997, p. 6). In this perspective, emotions are expressed and regulated in the context of interpersonal relationships; for example, in early infancy, emotional expression would often occur during parent-infant interactions, including both playful games and caregiving activities such as feeding or bathing the infants.

More broadly, dynamic systems theories focus on the context surrounding individuals' actions and expressions of emotion in the course of interactions with familiar and unfamiliar people. Working within this tradition, the theorists Geert and Steenbeek noted that the English word 'development' itself has evolved from the early French word *desvoloper* which means 'to unwrap' (Geert & Steenbeek, 2005). We can picture the developmental process as unfolding a rolled-up sleeping bag. Using mathematical equations to represent change over time, the dynamic systems theorists model how psychological or developmental states at Time 1 transform into states at Time 2, which in turn transform into a new state as an interaction continue or as a child grows older. In other words, while much of developmental psychology focuses on individual continuity over the course of development, the dynamic theorists use mathematics to track the changes over time.

Neurobiological Theories

In the 21st century, with the development of new technologies to explore brain functions, biologists and psychologists have drawn attention to the neurobiological contributions to different emotions and some parallels between human beings' emotional experience and those of other species, including positive as well as negative emotions (e.g., Burgdorf & Panksepp, 2006). One area of controversy is whether the primary emotions such as anger, fear, sadness, and happiness are generated by localized areas of the brain and specific patterns of brain function (Primary Emotion Theory), or whether neurobiological structures and processes support the general experience of feeling emotions and perceiving the emotions in others (Psychological Construction Theory).

In Primary Emotion Theory, different primary emotions are thought to be associated with specific brain regions. For example, anger is thought to be associated with the orbitofrontal cortex, fear with the amygdala, and sadness with the medial prefrontal cortex. In contrast, Psychological Construction Theories do not focus on links between the primary emotions and specific brain regions; rather, from this perspective, theorists consider general features of emotion that are not limited to specific emotions, such as general links between the expression of emotion and past experience and the patterns of individual differences that may be influenced by cultural factors (Burgdoff & Panksepp, 2006).

Further Reading

Hay, D. F. (2019). *Emotional development from childhood to adolescence*. London: Routledge.
Jarvis, M. (2000). *Theoretical approaches in psychology*. London: Routledge.
Slater, A., & Quinn, P. C. (2021). *Developmental psychology: Revisiting the classic studies*. London: Sage.
Sroufe, L. A. (1995). *Emotional development: The organization of emotional life in the early years*. Cambridge: Cambridge University Press.

References

Ainsworth, M. D. S. (1969). Object relations, dependency, and attachment: A theoretical review of the infant-mother relationship. *Child Development, 40*, 969–1025.
Ainsworth, M. D. S. (1985). Patterns of infant-mother attachments. *Bulletin of the New York Academy of Medicine, 61*, 775–776.
Ainsworth, M. D. S., Blehar, M., Waters, E., & Wall, S. (2015). *Patterns of attachment: A psychological study of the strange situation*. New York, NY: Psychology Press.
Bandura, A., & Walters, R. H. (1963). *Social learning and personality development*. New York, NY: Holt, Rinehart, & Winston.
Bekoff, M. (2005). *Animal passions and beastly virtues: Reflections on redecorating nature*. Philadelphia, PA: Temple University Press.
Blurton Jones, N. (1972). *Ethological studies of child behaviour*. Cambridge: Cambridge University Press.
Bowlby, J. (1969). *Attachment and loss*. London: Hogarth.
Bridges, K. (1932). Emotional development in early infancy. *Child Development, 3*, 324–341.
Burgdorf, J., & Panksepp, J. (2006). The neurobiology of positive emotions. *Neuroscience and Biobehavioral Reviews, 30*, 173–187.
Cole, P. (1986). Children's spontaneous control of facial expressions. *Child Development, 57*, 1309–1321.
Darwin, C. (1887). A biographical sketch of an infant. *Mind: A Quarterly Review of Psychology and Philosophy, 2*, 285–294.

Eibl-Eibesfeldt, I. (1979). Human ethology: Concepts and implications. *Behavioural and Brain Sciences*, 2, 1–26.

Ekman, P., & Friesen, W. V. (1978). *Facial Action Coding System (FACS)*. Palo Alto, CA: APA PsycTests.

Fogel, A., Dickson, K. L., Hsu, H. C., Messinger, D., Nelson-Goens, C., & Nwokah, E. (1997). Communication of smiling and laughing in mother-infant play: Research on emotion from a dynamic systems perspective. *New Directions for Child Development*, 77, 5–24.

Freud, S. (1920). *A general introduction to psychoanalysis*. New York, NY: Liveright.

Geert, P., & Steenbeek, H. (2005). Explaining after by before: Basic aspects of a dynamic systems approach to the study of development. *Developmental Review*, 25, 408–442.

Goodall, J. A. (1990). *Through a window: 30 years of observing the Gombe chimpanzees*. London: Weidenfeld and Nicolson.

Isaacs, S. (1968). *The nursery years: The mind of the child from birth to six years.* New York: Shocken Books, Inc.

Jersild, A. T. (1946). Emotional development. In L. Carmichael (Ed.), *Manual of child psychology* (pp. 752–790). New York, NY: Wiley.

Klein, M. (1952). The origins of transference. *International Journal of Psychoanalysis*, 33, 433–438.

Lindquist, D. H. (2020). Emotion in motion: A three-stage model of aversive classical conditioning. *Neuroscience and Biobehavioral Reviews*, 115, 363–377.

Moss, C. (2000). *Elephant memories: Thirteen years in the life of an elephant family.* Chicago: University of Chicago Press.

Murchison, C., & Langer, S. (1927). Tiedemann's observations on the development of the mental faculties of children. *The Pedagogical Seminary and Journal of Genetic Psychology*, 34, 205–230.

Pavlov, I. P. (1927). *Conditioned reflexes; An investigation of the physiological activity of the cerebral cortex* (G. V. Anrep, Trans). Oxford: Oxford University Press.

Ribot, T. (1903). *The general ideas of infants and deaf mutes: A psychological study.* New York, NY: C Appleton and Company.

Skinner, B. (1938). *The behavior of organisms.* New York, NY: Appleton-Century-Crofts.

Sroufe, L. A. (1995). *Emotional development: The organization of emotional life in the early years.* Cambridge: Cambridge University Press.

Tiedemann, D. (1787). Beobachtunger fiber die Entwicklung der Seetenfhrigkeiten Bei Kindern. *Hessischen Beitrage zur Gelehrsamkeit und Kunst*, 2, 313; 3, 486.

Watson, J. B., & Rayner, R. C. (1920). Conditioned emotional reactions. *Journal of Experimental Psychology*, 3, 1–14.

Chapter 3

Key Methods for Studying Emotional Development

Psychologists use a wide variety of research techniques to study children's emotional development. They have developed a variety of ways of designing studies, collecting data, and analysing the data that have been collected. The precise methods used have changed over time, profiting from the development of new technologies and the invention of novel research paradigms. However, psychologists who study emotional development still continue to use well-established research methods, as well as more recently invented techniques, to find answers to their research questions.

In this chapter, we shall look at different processes in carrying out a developmental study: design of the study to answer particular research questions; consideration of ethical issues; recruitment of an appropriate sample from a defined population; procedures used to collect data; and the measures developed to analyse all the different types of data that have been collected. Many different methods have been used in the studies described in this book. They include direct observation, informants' reports, experimental designs, standardized psychometric assessments, psychophysiology, and brain imaging. All of these techniques have been used to study different aspects of emotional development, which will become evident in the chapters that follow. First, though, it is helpful to examine the methods that have yielded so much information about children's emotions.

Designing Studies of Children's Emotional Development

Several different research designs that have been featured in different areas of psychological research have also been used to study children's emotional development. Some types of research on emotional development require the study of large, representative populations. Other studies focus on smaller groups of children whose experiences may provide unique insights into the features and stages of emotional development.

DOI: 10.4324/9781003483793-4

Experimental studies examine children's immediate reactions to emotional challenges. Despite this diversity of research designs, all studies of children's emotions must consider the age-appropriateness of the study, the ethics of the procedures, and the suitability of the measures for children at that age being studied. One of the first decisions developmental researchers must make is to decide whether they will use a cross-sectional design (comparing children from different age groups) or a longitudinal design that measures the same children at different points in time. Both types of design are used in the study of emotional development.

Cross-sectional Studies of Emotional Expression and Understanding

Cross-sectional studies compare children of different ages, thus providing information about age differences in patterns of emotional expression and the levels of emotional understanding that emerge at different time points in children's lives. Such comparisons of children of different ages help psychologists to identify the points in development when children begin to express particular emotions and then begin to interpret and respond to other people's emotions.

In cross-sectional studies, the parents or other caregivers of children of different ages are asked for their permission to let their children participate in a study of age differences in emotion expression or emotion understanding. Such studies are often conducted in primary schools where the researchers can compare year groups. For example, if you were conducting a study of children's recognition of different emotions as shown in photographs, you might compare four-year-olds with three-year-olds and five-year-olds.

Cross-sectional studies like this often recruit children who are in primary schools and then compare the emotional skills and emotional understanding in different year groups. For example, in a study of children in Chinese primary schools, children's abilities to recognize emotions in videos of adult actors were observed (Wang, Hawk, Tang, Schlegel, & Zou, 2019). Different year groups in the school, at the average ages of 8, 9, 10, 11, and 12 years, were compared in the cross-sectional design. Even the youngest children could recognize joy and anger but were less likely to recognize other emotions expressed by the adults in the videos.

Cross-sectional Designs

Research designs for developmental studies that compare children or adolescents who are members of different age groups and are observed at the same time. Cross-sectional designs measure age differences but do not reveal changes over time.

Longitudinal Studies of Emotional Development

Cross-sectional studies have provided much important information about emotional expressions and emotional skills in different age groups, but they cannot reveal how children's emotions develop and change over time. In contrast, in longitudinal studies, the same individuals are studied repeatedly over time, and the investigators analyse the ways in which they change—for example, as children grow older, they do not just express their emotions non-verbally by crying or laughing but can describe how they feel. It's important to note that longitudinal research designs explore continuity as well as change; some children are temperamentally more emotional than others right from the start, and in longitudinal studies that consistency in their emotional life can be traced over time. Thus, longitudinal designs allow us to see how children become their unique selves over time, manifesting their stable personalities while growing older and tackling new challenges.

> **Longitudinal Designs**
>
> Developmental research designs that follow a cohort of infants, children, or adolescents born in the same time period as they grow older over time. Some studies of ageing also use longitudinal designs.

Longitudinal studies on emotional development have revealed both change and continuity in their samples. For example, in The Child and Parent Emotion Study (Westrupp, MacDonald, Bennett, et al., 2020), over 2000 families from six different countries were studied repeatedly over 12 years, starting during the mothers' pregnancies. The investigators collected information about the emotional climates in the different families, the parents' approaches to emotional socialization, and the development of children's abilities to regulate their own emotions. In that study, the investigators examined parents' reactions to their children's emotions over time, comparing those parents who were disengaged from the children's emotions, those who dismissed the children's expressions of emotions, and those who used 'emotion coaching' to help children understand and express their feelings. The investigators found that the children of parents who were disengaged or dismissive of the children's emotional experiences were more likely to develop mental health problems as they grew older (Frogley, King, & Westrupp, 2023). These findings illustrate the ways in which longitudinal designs allow the study of developmental change while also identifying individual differences that persist over time.

Experimental designs. Some investigators have studied emotional development using experimental designs that compare different groups of children who have had different experiences. They might conduct a true randomized experiment where the participants are randomly assigned to different conditions (e.g., an experimental group who have experienced one set of conditions and a comparison group who do not have that experience). For example, the experimental group may see or hear something that is frightening, but the comparison group may see or hear something that is pleasant or neutral. In a true experiment, children are randomly assigned to one group or the other, so that they do not differ on anything except the experimental protocol being used in the study.

Experimental designs that focus on children's emotions raise ethical questions. Is it ethically sound to frighten children or manipulate the situation in a way that makes them sad or angry? Is it fair that children in the experimental group have such an emotionally different experience compared to the comparison group? Researchers and ethical review boards must decide whether it's ethically acceptable to manipulate children's emotions in a laboratory setting. In other words, could this manipulation have lasting effects on children's well-being?

As we shall see in the following chapters, various experimental paradigms have been approved for use to study children's emotional reactions. The results of those studies have had an important impact on theories of emotional development. These experimental studies include the Strange Situation, a procedure used in the study of infants' attachments to their parents and other caregivers (see Chapter 3). Experimental studies have also been designed to study children's reactions to people and things that might frighten them, such as the 'visual cliff' procedure, when infants are given the chance to crawl across a transparent surface that is completely solid but has been made to look as if the infants might fall off the surface (see Chapter 3).

More recent studies may use experimental methods to foster positive emotions. For example, in one experimental study, four-year-old children who lived in disadvantaged circumstances were encouraged to engage in pretend play games where they took on the roles of people or animals who expressed emotions in different emotionally relevant scenarios (Goldstein & Lerner, 2018). The investigators reported that the children in the experimental condition who engaged in pretend play were more likely to control their emotions later on.

Natural experiments. In some other studies of emotional development, groups of children are compared, but their belonging to one group rather than another has not been random. Rather, the two groups of children have had very different experiences that create what scientists call a 'natural experiment': two or more groups in such studies have had very different experiences in childhood. For example, some studies compare individuals who had lived in orphanages or other residential institutions with a comparison group of children who had lived with their parents in family homes. Other studies compare children who have lived in war zones with children who have not been exposed to armed conflict. Still other research compares children who have experienced natural disasters like earthquakes or tornados with children who did not have such frightening experiences. Children who experience such devastating events may develop different types of emotional processing and different ways to regulate their own emotions.

Recruiting Samples

Several types of samples have been used in the study of children's emotional development. Cross-sectional studies involve sampling individuals from different age groups; such studies often compare children of different ages by recruiting participants from different classrooms in a primary school or childcare setting. In contrast, in longitudinal studies, investigators recruit a sample of families who consent to participate more than once at different points in time. In cross-sectional studies of emotional development, groups of children of different ages are compared with each other in relation to their expression and understanding of emotions. They are tested once and typically not followed up at older ages. In contrast, in longitudinal studies of emotional development, a sample of children is recruited and those children are studied over time. In other words, cross-sectional studies examine *age groups* at one point in time; longitudinal studies follow up a single sample over time. In longitudinal studies, the investigators measure changes in children's expression and understanding of their own and other people's emotions as they grow older. However, longitudinal studies provide the opportunity to measure continuity as well as change in children's expression of emotion over time. In longitudinal studies, individual differences in the expression and understanding of emotion can be tracked over time.

When recruiting participants for their studies, investigators must decide whether to recruit any children and families who happen to volunteer to participate or whether to focus on a sample from a well-defined population. For example, in the large, longitudinal national cohort studies undertaken in the UK, such as the UK Millennial Cohort Study (MCS), the population is defined beforehand. In the case of MCS, the sample was drawn from all the children in the UK who were born at the turn of the new millennium (Connelly & Platt, 2014).

Population-based studies might also target children who live in a particular community, such as the study that began in the 1960s, focusing on all the families with 10-year-olds living on the Isle of Wight (e.g., Maughan, Rutter, & Yule, 2020). Once the population that is being sampled from has been defined, the investigators attempt to recruit a sample that is fully representative of that population. For example, in a longitudinal study of firstborn infants born in two UK National Health Service districts in Wales, the research team recruited participating families who were attending prenatal clinics in hospitals or GP practices (Hay et al., 2021). Subsequent analyses showed that the sample obtained was representative of the UK as a whole.

However, many studies of children's emotional development have drawn *samples of convenience* from a school or childcare centre that is happy to contribute to research on children's development. This approach is particularly appropriate for studies in which children are asked to take part in observational studies or experimental tasks that can be easily administered in sessions in a child development laboratory or in the familiar settings of the children's schools and childcare centres.

Different Ways to Measure Children's Emotions

Our feelings are not always visible; indeed, adults may often try to suppress or disguise their emotions. Infants and young children are more blatant in their expressions of emotion, but even then, there are nuances in their emotional outbursts—for example, infants express their displeasure with different types of cries, depending on the situations they are in and the reasons for their distress. Investigators have used different types of age- and situation-appropriate methods to measure children's emotions. They carry out their studies in participants' homes, in schools, and in research laboratories. They may also administer questionnaires to participants either online or by mail. Here are some of the research methods and particular techniques that have been used to study children's emotional development.

Observational Methods

Baby biographies. Some of the earliest observational studies of children's development took the form of adults' diaries of children's early development, as illustrated earlier by Darwin's precise observations of his son Doddy. Philosophers and poets, as well as parents and other family members, recorded young infants' behaviours in their diaries. These diarists included the German philosopher Friedrich Tiedemann in the 18th century and the English poet Samuel Coleridge in the early 19th century, as well as later

Baby Biographies

Detailed observations of infants and young children written in diaries by parents and other relatives. Samuel Coleridge, Charles Darwin, Friedrich Tiedemann, amongst other scholars and scientists, wrote baby biographies in the 18th and 19th centuries that recorded infants' emotions and skills, which were later studied in larger samples.

scientists, fathers, and aunts in the late 19th and early 20th centuries. These biographies of individual children provide useful qualitative data on infants' and young children's abilities and emotions.

Observations of social interactions in children's classrooms. More systematic observational studies began to be conducted in nursery schools, especially in Canada and the United States where several centres for early education had been funded by the Rockefeller Foundation. A number of early observational studies of children's development took place in those scientifically funded nursery schools, including key observational studies on the development of children's expressions of their emotions (e.g., Bridges, 1932). These investigators often made direct observations of children in nursery schools and on playgrounds.

Subsequent studies of children's emotions in the later decades of the 20th century devised standardized procedures in laboratory studies. Other studies relied on reports by parents, teachers and other people in children's lives, via interviews or questionnaires, and children's own self-reports of their emotional experience. Longitudinal studies have traced the development of children's emotions over time. In recent years, the methods for studying emotional development have been expanded to include physiological measurement, brain imaging, and genetic analyses.

Measurement

The types of measurement that are used in studies of emotional development often depend on the sample size. In very large samples of families drawn from nationally representative populations, the investigators are likely to use well-established, standardized questionnaires completed by parents or teachers rather than more time-consuming observational or experimental methods. In such large samples, it is rare for children's own voices to be heard. However, in smaller samples, it is feasible to observe children in their homes or schools or set up experimental tasks that might be responded to with different emotions.

Some studies of emotional development use well-established standardized procedures such as emotion recognition tests that use photographs of adults or children expressing specific emotions. In other studies, infants and young children may be challenged by unfamiliar environments. For example, in the measure of attachment quality known as the Strange Situation (Ainsworth et al., 2015), a task was designed to measure infants' emotional reactions to the presence of strangers and brief separations from their parents. Studies of somewhat older children have set up experiments where children become frustrated or fearful in unfamiliar or otherwise challenging environments.

Because there are so many different methods used in studying emotional development, the findings about the development of any emotion will vary across the populations that are being sampled, the methodological decisions made by the investigators, and the types of measures they use.

Approaches to Data Analysis

As we have seen, many psychological studies of emotional development may compare groups of children of different ages (cross-sectional designs) or study the same sample of children over time (longitudinal designs). The different designs require different ways of analysing data. Simple cross-sectional studies that compare two or more age groups are likely to measure differences between well-defined age groups, using statistics such as t-tests, analysis of variance, or, if other factors are being controlled for, analyses of covariance. Longitudinal studies are more likely to examine both change and continuity over time. *Change* will be examined by tracing the patterns of key variables, such as measures of fear or sadness, increasing or decreasing or fading away entirely as a child grows older. *Continuities* in emotional development will be detected by examining individual differences that are stable over time, so that the child's emotional expression at one point (e.g., fear of an unfamiliar person) predicts the same emotional responses at a later age (e.g., fear of venturing into a new situation, such as starting school for the first time). Children's ways of expressing their emotions, as well as their understanding of other people's emotions, will change over time, as they grow older and learn more about the world. However, some emotional patterns that emerge in the early years may predict aspects of children's emotional lives years later.

Clinical Definitions

In this book, we are not only looking at general trends in emotional development but are also examining the body of findings on individual differences in children's feelings and their expressions of emotion. These individual differences include the early variations in individuals' temperaments in infancy and childhood and also the development of different forms of emotional problems in childhood and adolescence. Studies of emotional development draw upon a complex literature, where different investigators have used various ways of measuring features of children's temperaments and signs of emotional problems. Emotion researchers use direct observations, standardized questionnaires and laboratory assessments, and sometimes all three in a given study.

However, when making formal clinical diagnoses, clinicians tend to use one of two diagnostic systems, either the International Classification of Diseases (ICD), which is used more often in European samples, or the Diagnostic and Statistical Manual (DSM), which was developed primarily

Diagnostic Systems

Sets of definitions used to diagnose mental health problems in children and adults, agreed upon by panels of experts, which are used both in clinical practice and in research on mental health. Two frequently used diagnostic systems are the *International Classification of Diseases (ICD)* and the *Diagnostic and Statistical Manual (DSM)*; each of these systems has been updated several times.

for North American samples and has since been used internationally. In the chapters that follow, the diagnostic system that was used in a given study will be noted. However, to be consistent with the majority of studies whose findings are being discussed, the DSM definitions of the symptoms of emotional disorders in childhood will be presented in tables that show how diagnoses are made.

Ethical Dilemmas

Studies of children's development always raise ethical questions and dilemmas, and that is particularly true when studying emotional development. For example, when psychologists began studying the development of fear, they set up challenging scenarios that might frighten children and might frighten some children more than others. The proposals for all future studies must undergo scrutiny by ethics committees, and the study protocols must ensure that children and their families are treated ethically.

The ethical issues that must be kept in mind when beginning a study include confidentiality (the participants' identities should never be revealed and all efforts must be taken to anonymize the findings). Informed consent is imperative; it requires not only permission from parents but also the actual consent of the children themselves. If children wish to stop participating in an experiment, the experimenter must take their feelings seriously and stop the procedure.

In the chapters that follow, we will consider some of the specific ethical issues in the study of different emotions and consider whether children are properly protected from adverse emotional outcomes. Ethical protocols must be developed long before participants take part in the studies, and ethical considerations need to be kept in mind at all stages of the study, from its design to the reporting of findings.

Further Reading

Darling-Churchill, K. E., & Lippman, L. (2016). Early childhood and emotional development: Advancing the field of measurement. *Journal of Applied Developmental Psychology*, 45, 1–7.

Halle, T. G., & Darling-Churchill, K. E. (2016). Review of measures of social and emotional development. *Journal of Applied Developmental Psychology, 45*, 8–18.
Mukherji, P., & Alban, D. (2022). *Research methods in early childhood: An introductory guide.* London: Sage.

References

Ainsworth, M. D. S., Blehar, M., Waters, E., & Wall, S. (2015). *Patterns of attachment: A psychological study of the strange situation.* New York, NY: Psychology Press.

Bridges, K. M. B. (1932). Emotional development in early infancy. *Child Development,* 324–341.

Connolly, R., & Platt, L. (2014). Cohort profile: UK Millennium Cohort Study (MCS). *International Journal of Epidemiology, 43,* 1719–1725.

Frogley, W. J., King, G. L., & Westrupp, E. M. (2023). Profiles of parent emotion socialization: Longitudinal associations with child emotional outcomes. *Mental Health and Prevention, 30,* 200274.

Goldstein, T. R., & Lerner, M. D. (2018). Dramatic pretend play games uniquely improve emotional control in young children. *Developmental Science, 21*(4), e12603.

Hay, D. F., Paine, A. L., Perra, O., Cook, K. V., Hashmi, S., Robinson, C., Kairis, V., & Slade, R. (2021). Prosocial and aggressive behavior: A longitudinal study. *Monographs of the Society for Research in Child Development, 86*(2), 7–103.

Maughan, B., Rutter, M., & Yule, W. (2020). The Isle of Wight studies: The scope and scale of reading difficulties. *Oxford Review of Education, 46,* 429–438.

Wang, Y., Hawk, S. T., Tang, Y., Schlegel, K., & Zou, H. (2019). Characteristics of emotion recognition ability among primary school children: Relationships With peer status and friendship quality. *Springer Nature Link, 12,* 1369–1388.

Westrupp, E., MacDonald, J. A., Bennett, C., Havighurst, S., Kehoe, C. E., Foley, D., Berkowitz, T. S., King, G. L., & Youseff, G. J. (2020). The child and parent emotion study: Protocol for a longitudinal study of parent emotion socialisation and child socioemotional development. *BMJ Open, 10,* e03812.

Key Emotions and Empirical Findings

In Section 2, you will learn about the development of different emotions and the developmental pathways that may lead some children to experience clinically significant emotional disorders. Section 2 is organized in pairs of chapters. The first chapter in each pair describes the development of a primary emotion, with the paired chapter then describing how individual differences in that emotion may in some cases lead to an emotional disorder. The order of the chapters in Section 2 reflects the ages at which children begin to express these different emotions.

By the end of Section 2, you will have learnt about:

- Infants' first expressions of emotion, which begin with *crying* but soon followed by *smiling and laughing.*
- The development of children's experiences of the primary emotions of *fear* and *disgust.*
- Some children's experiences of clinically significant problems related to those emotions, including *extreme fear, anxiety,* and *phobias.*
- The development of the primary emotion of *anger* in infancy and early childhood.
- The emergence of *individual differences* in children's anger, leading to some children showing *difficult temperament, angry aggressiveness,* and *oppositional defiant disorder.*
- The early development of the social emotion of *empathy* in childhood and the absence of empathy and sympathy in some children who are callous toward other people's problems. Such callousness may develop into clinically significant *conduct disorder.*
- The development of the primary emotion of *sadness* and the emergence of individual differences in children who experience *dislocation, loss, and bereavement.*
- The biological, social, and environmental factors that may trigger *clinical depression* in children and adolescents.

DOI: 10.4324/9781003483793-5

Chapter 4

Expressing Feelings
Infants' Crying, Smiling, and Laughing

Crying

The very first thing a newborn infant does is cry. An infant's first cry is a welcome sound to the parents and any other people present at the birth, a triumphant noise that proclaims that the infant is alive and has successfully travelled out of the mother's body into the outside world. Newborn crying is informative, telling the world about the infant's immediate discomfort, and as such, crying is a compelling signal to the mother as she holds her child for the first time. Already the infant's cry has become a mode of communication to the mother and other caregivers. Crying is an expression of discomfort that becomes more nuanced over the first months of life.

Infants' crying is both universal—all infants cry—but also individual—there are individual differences in crying from birth onwards, and parents soon begin to recognize the distinct features of their own infant's cry.

Crying is not just important for human infants. Members of other species also express distress vocally. Human infants cry when they are hungry, cold, or in pain, communicating their immediate needs; members of other mammalian species similarly tend to vocalize when experiencing hunger, cold, or pain (Lingle, Wyman, Kotrba, Teichraeb, & Romanow, 2012). For example, young chimpanzees cry for long periods of time when they find themselves at a distance from their mothers (Bard, 2000). Evolutionary biologists have suggested that such 'callback' cries may have evolved in different species as a protective signal for infants who may wander away from their mothers (Cecchini, Lai, & Langher, 2007). Crying is a critical channel of communication for infants.

Callback Cries

Young primates' distressed crying when they've been separated from their mothers.

Parents often report that over the course of a day, their infants may cry in different ways, depending on their needs and circumstances. Infants

DOI: 10.4324/9781003483793-6

Acoustic Jitter

Quick variations in infants' crying frequencies, when combined with high pitch, signal distress that is aversive to listeners, who may try to respond more quickly to the infants' needs.

Cry Signatures

Infants express individually distinct cries when they are distressed; however, pain cries are less individual.

who are experiencing pain are more likely to emit high-pitched cries; for example, infant boys being circumcised produce very high-pitched cries of pain (Porter, Miller, & Marshall, 1986). Infants in pain also vary the pitch of their cries, producing sounds that acoustic scientists call 'jitter'; cries that combine high pitch and jitter are very aversive to adults who may then respond as quickly as possible to the crying infants (Protopapas & Eimas, 1997).

All these common features of crying have powerful effects on the adults who are listening, but infants' crying is also highly individual: infants have distinctive 'cry signatures' that their parents can recognize (Gustafson, Sanborn, Lin, & Green, 2017). Furthermore, different infants cry at different rates. Some cry more often and for longer periods than others. Crying is a powerful signal that communicates urgency. Individual differences in frequency of bouts of crying, the length of time infants spend crying, and the acoustic qualities of their cries will all affect the parents' own emotional states.

Smiling and Laughing

Infants' vocal communications are not always about being upset. They begin to smile and express other signs of contentment in their first months of life. Infants' smiles and laughter are important signals to their parents and other caregivers, another way to communicate with the adults who look after them. Furthermore, even if infants are neither smiling nor laughing, they are likely to be focusing their attention on the people around them, taking an interest in and expressing enjoyment of the connections they are making with other people (Reddy, 2019).

Psychologists began to study infants' positive emotions in more depth in the early 20th century. For example, Washburn (1929) observed 15 infants (9 girls and 6 boys) once a month over the first year of life. Infants' smiles were observed by 12 weeks of age. Their laughter was first heard some time later, and the investigators reported that laughing was more stereotyped than smiling. But even in that very small sample, individual differences were already present. Some infants smiled and laughed more than others; some were generally less expressive, smiling (but also crying) less often than the other infants.

Subsequent studies of smiling and laughter in infancy have focused on the patterns of individual differences as well as general developmental changes over time. Some studies of the development of smiling and laughing measure the social dynamics of infants' interactions with parents and other familiar adults, recording the ways in which infants and the adults who care for them smile and laugh.

Infants' Smiles

Infants smile even before they are born. Ultrasound technology has revealed infants' smiling while they are still floating in their mothers' wombs (Reissland et al., 2011). At this early stage of prenatal development, smiling is thought to be reflexive, a sign of homeostasis and not yet a social signal. Even after being born, infants' early smiles reflect their physical well-being. Smiles occur when the infants are not experiencing any internal discomfort and might be seen as a prenatal sign of contentment. Newborn infants even smile in their sleep (Dondi et al., 2007; Emde & Koenig, 1969).

Infants' earliest smiles are simple, just an upturning of their lips, which they had been doing even before they were born. Sometimes, in the first months, infants turn up their lips while simultaneously dropping their jaw. That expression, which is also seen in some non-human primates, has been called a 'play smile' (Bolzani et al., 2002). The use of this term suggests that human infants as well as other primates produce playful smiles when they are having fun. However, in infancy, play smiles may not yet be a deliberate act to communicate an infant's feelings to another person; some jaw dropping has already been observed in ultrasound pictures of foetal mouth movements when the infant is still in the mother's womb (Reissland, Francis, Aydin, Mason, & Exley, 2014).

Play Smiles

Smiles in which infants turn up their lips while dropping their jaws; these do not necessarily occur during infant-parent interaction but are also shown during solitary play.

Over the first months after birth, smiling gradually becomes a way for infants to communicate with other people. They are now able to combine gazing at another person with simple smiles, turning up their lips as they had been doing even before they were born. The development of smiling is partly influenced by a development of the nervous system termed the

Duchenne Smiles

Smiles that are produced by two sets of muscles, not only the contraction of the zygomatic major muscles that raise the corners of the lips, but also the contraction of the orbicularis oculi that crinkles the skin around the eyes.

'two-month shift' combined with the experience of face-to-face interactions with their primary caregivers (Wormann, Holodynski, Kartner, & Keller, 2012). However, the ability to smile is not simply a function of the infant's maturing nervous system but also a product of social interaction.

Somewhat later in the first year, infants make facial expressions that are called 'full smiles' (also known as 'Duchenne smiles'), which occur most often in social situations when the infants are gazing at other people. To produce full smiles, an infant must move two facial muscles simultaneously, the zygomatic major, which pulls up the corners of the lips, and the orbicularis oculi, pars lateralis, which makes the infants squint their eyes and raise their cheeks (Bolzani, Messinger, Yale, & Dondi, 2002).

Duply Smiles

Infants' smiles that combine the features of play smiles with Duchenne smiles, i.e., smiles that combine raised lips with dropped jaws.

Infants are especially likely to produce full smiles when they are interacting with their parents or other familiar caregivers. Occasionally, infants may combine their play smiles (where they drop their jaws) with their full Duchenne smiles; this combination is referred to as a *duply smile* (Fogel, Nelson-Goens, Hsu, & Shapiro, 2000). Thus, even in the early months, infants' smiles both express their inner states of enjoyment and provide a means of interacting with others, especially with their parents and other caregivers. Before infants produce their first words, they are likely to combine speech-like sounds with the production of wide Duchenne smiles (Hsu, Fogel, & Messinger, 2001).

Around the time of their first birthdays, infants begin to use different types of smiles in different contexts, such as various types of social games. In one study (Fogel et al., 2000), 6- and 12-month-olds' smiling was recorded during two types of games played with their mothers: the *visual* game of peekaboo in which the players hide their faces, which is played at a distance, and a *tactile* game in which the mothers tickle their infants. The investigators found no significant differences between girls and boys or between the 6- and 12-month-olds. Rather, the infants smiled throughout the study from the time they entered the laboratory through all the different experimental procedures. However, the type of game affected the type of smiles they produced. The infants produced more Duchenne smiles and duply smiles when they were being tickled than when they were playing peekaboo at a distance.

This finding supports the view that when young infants smile during games with their parents and other caregivers, they are expressing genuine enjoyment and playfulness. Indeed, the adults playing with the infants also smile and laugh, expressing the good humour that adults and infants both experience while playing with each other (Reddy, 2003). However, there are some cultural differences in the extent to which parents and infants play in this way. For example, a longitudinal comparison of mothers' and infants' mutual smiling in two samples, one recruited in Germany and the other in Cameroon, revealed some differences between the samples. Mother-infant smiling games were similar in the two samples when the infants were six months of age but had diverged by their first birthday (Wormann et al., 2012). This suggests that developmental trends in infants' smiling and laughing are not simply due to physical maturation but are influenced by social experiences in diverse cultures.

Laughing

For human infants, laughing is a sign of sociability and a feature of positive social interactions (Reddy, 2003). Smiling requires infants to move their facial muscles; to laugh, they must use their lungs as well, inhaling and exhaling to produce gleeful sounds. Laughter is also sociable and communicative, emerging long before infants can communicate with words. Most infants start laughing around four months of age (Mireault et al., 2014), although they may try to laugh earlier; some sounds that resemble a laugh are produced as early as two months of age (Rothbart, 1973).

Young infants laugh in response to being touched, for example, when they're being tickled or given a buzzy kiss on their stomachs (Mireault et al., 2015). They also laugh when the adults around them make funny sounds (Sroufe & Waters, 1976). Some scholars have suggested that laughter has evolved in other mammalian species as well as humans. For example, the great apes exhale during social play; young infants similarly laugh while exhaling (Kret, Venneker, Evans, Samara, & Sauter, 2021). Even young rats produce subvocal sounds during rough-and-tumble play (Panksepp & Burgdorf, 2003).

Laughter is not only expressive of one's inner emotional state but also a mode of communication with other people. For example, in an intensive longitudinal study where infants and mothers were observed weekly during the first year and every other week for the next two years, both mothers' and infants' laughter was recorded (Nwokah, Hsu, Dobrowolska, & Fogel, 1994). The infants in that sample began to laugh in the first year, between 10 and 21 weeks of age. Their initial laughs were short, and mothers were not always sure that the infants were in fact laughing, but the duration of infant laughter increased over that first year. Increasingly, over the first two years, mothers and infants engaged in simultaneous laughter.

Social Referencing

Interactions in which infants who are in a new place or have been presented with a novel object look to their parents or other caregivers for cues before they respond emotionally to the situation. For example, if an unfamiliar person comes into the room, infants might look to their parents' faces to check how they should respond to the newcomer.

Infants' Clowning

Infants' intentional acts that make their parents and other caregivers laugh.

Even in infancy, laughing along with another person is underpinned by the 'social referencing' that infants engage in with their parents and other familiar people (Reddy, 2003). Eye-tracking studies have shown that infants are already turning to look to their parents' faces for information by six months of age. Although social referencing has often been studied in relation to infants' potentially fearful responses to novel situations (see Chapter 3), young infants look to their caregivers' faces for emotional cues while they engage in social games. Furthermore, in the first year of life, infants not only laugh, but they also try to get their companions to laugh as well. They begin to engage in 'clowning,' doing things that elicit laughter from their parents and other adults, just as their parents have done to get the infants to laugh in the early months (Reddy & Mireault, 2014). Thus, smiling and laughing underpin infants' playful interactions with their parents and other familiar people. By the last quarter of the first year, infants take pleasure in playing social games with others, exchanging objects back and forth and hiding and revealing their faces in games of peekaboo (e.g., Ross & Lollis, 1989). Thus, by the time they reach their first birthdays, infants are adept at expressing humour and enjoyment as well as communicating their distress to their caregivers.

Contagious Crying

It has long been observed that when one infant cries, other infants may begin to cry as well (Darwin, 1887; Preyer, 1889). Contagious crying has been observed in the first days of life (Sagi & Hoffman, 1976; Simner, 1971). Evolutionary theorist Frans de Waal (2008) has proposed that emotional contagion is an evolved social phenomenon that is present in the great apes as well as human infants. Some psychologists have proposed that infants' emotional responses to other infants' cries are one of the first steps in the development of empathy (Davidov et al., 2013).

Some sceptics have suggested that the infants get confused

Contagious Crying

Infants' crying that occurs in response to other infants' cries, sometimes leading to a group of infants all crying at once.

between their own distress and the sounds produced by other infants; however, experiments have shown that infants can discriminate between recordings of their own crying and the crying of other infants (Dondi et al., 1999).

It has also been proposed that contagious crying is an early form of imitation (Simner, 1971). However, it is also possible that the sound of crying is simply an annoying noise that other infants find upsetting and cry when they hear it. Even newborns may begin to cry when they hear other infants cry (Simner, 1971; Sagi & Hoffman, 1976). This could be interpreted as the infants' negative reactions to crying as a noxious sound, not a sign of sympathetic concern. However, observations of infants as young as six months of age have shown that when infants cry, other infants most often watch their distressed peers, only gradually becoming distressed themselves; they also look toward the sad peers' mothers, not their own mothers, as they presumably would do if they were experiencing personal distress (Hay et al., 1981; Liddle et al., 2015). In one study, when infants were shown a video of a crying infant, they most often showed their concern for the distressed infant via gestures and facial expressions, not by becoming distressed themselves (Roth-Hanania et al., 2011). These gestures and expressions are even shown by three-month-olds who are watching distressed infants (Davidov et al., 2020). All of these observations suggest that, for most children, concerned reactions to other people's distress begin to emerge in the first two years of life.

Beyond the clear evidence for contagious crying, young infants are attentive to other people's distress in other ways. Infants watch their distressed peers until they become upset themselves; the longer one infant cries, the more likely another infant will begin to cry as well (Hay, Nash, & Pedersen, 1981).

Infants are also sensitive to their mothers' simulated distress (Roth-Hanania, 2011). Infants react to their mothers' distress when they are only two months old (Davidov, Paz, et al., 2020). Taken together, all these findings suggest that infants are sensitive to and sometimes upset by other people's distress.

Some psychologists have asked whether such emotional contagion occurs for laughing as well as crying. Although parents and infants exchange smiles during their positive interactions, contagious laughter appears to be far less common than contagious crying in infancy (Jordan & Thomas, 2017). However, as children grow older, their social laughter is evident in some circumstances. For example, children are more likely to laugh at comic videos when they are with other children than when they are watching the videos on their own (Addyman, Fogelquist, Levakova, & Rees, 2018). Joint laughter is one of the most pleasurable social experiences in childhood.

Further Reading

Addyman, C. (2020). *The laughing baby: The extraordinary science behind what makes babies happy.* London: Unbound.

Vermillet, A.-Q., Tøllbøll, K., Mizan, S. L., Skewes, J. C., & Parsons, C. E. (2022). Crying in the first 12 months of life: A systematic review and meta-analysis of cross-country parent-reported data and modelling of the 'cry curve.' *Child Development, 93,* 1201–1222.

References

Addyman, C., Fogelquist, C., Levakova, L., & Rees, S. (2018). Social facilitation of laughter and smiles in preschool children. *Frontiers in Psychology, 9,* 1048.

Bard, K. (2000). In R. G. Barr, B. Hopkins, & J. A. Green (Eds.), *Crying as a sign, a symptom, and a signal: Aspects of infant and toddler crying.* New York, NY: Springer.

Bolzani, L. H., Messinger, D. S., Yale, M., & Dondi, M. (2002). Smiling in infancy. In M. H. Abel (Ed.), *The smile: Forms, functions, and consequences.* London: Mellen Press.

Cecchini, M., Lai, C., & Langher, V. (2007). Communication and crying in newborns. *Infant Behavior and Development, 30,* 655–665.

Darwin, C. (1887). A biographical sketch of an infant. *Mind: A Quarterly Review of Psychology and Philosophy, 2,* 285–294.

Davidov, M., Zahn-Waxler, C., Roth-Hanania, R., & Knafo, A. (2013). Concern for others in the first year of life: Theories, evidence, and avenues for research. *Child Development Perspectives, 7,* 126–131.

Davidov, M., Paz, Y., Roth-Hanania, R., Usefovsky, F., Orlitsky, T., Mankuta, D., & Zahn-Waxler, C. (2021). Caring babies: Concern for others in distress during infancy. *Developmental Science, 24,* e13016.

Dondi, M., Messinger, D., Colle, M., Tabasso, A., Simion, F., Barba, B. D., & Fogel, A. (2007). A new perspective on neonatal smiling: Differences between the judgments between the expert coders and naïve observers. *Infancy, 12,* 235–255.

Emde, R. N., & Koenig, E. L. (1969). Neonatal smiling and rapid eye movement states. *Journal of the American Academy of Child Psychiatry, 8,* 57–67.

Fogel, A., Nelson-Goens, G. C., Hsu, H.-C., & Shapiro, A. F. (2000). Do different infant smiles reflect different positive emotions? *Social Development, 9,* 497–520.

Gustafson, G. E., Sanborn, S. M., Lin, H.-C., & Green, J. A. (2017). Newborns' cries are unique to individuals (but not to language environment). *Infancy, 22,* 736–747.

Hay, D. F., Nash, A., & Pedersen, J. (1981). Responses of six-month-olds to the distress of their peers. *Child Development, 52,* 1071–1076.

Jordan, E. M., & Thomas, D. G. (2017). Contagious positive affective responses to laughter in infancy. *Archives of Psychology, 1,* 1–21.

Kret, M. E., Venneker, D., Evans, B., Samara, I., & Sauter, D. (2021). The ontogeny of human laughter. *Biology Letters, 17,* 20210319.

Liddle, M., Bradley, B. S., & McGrath, A. (2015). Baby empathy: Infant distress and peer prosocial responses. *Infant Mental Health, 36,* 446–458.

Lingle, S., Wyman, M. T., Kotrba, R., Teichraeb, L. J., & Romanow, C. A. (2012). What makes a cry a cry? A review of infant distress vocalizations. *Current Zoology, 58,* 698–726.

Mireault, G. C., Crockenberg, S., Sparrow, J. E., Pettinato, C. A., Woodard, K. C., & Malzac, K. (2014). Social looking, social referencing, and humor perception in 6- and 12-month-old infants. *Infant Behavior and Development, 17,* 536–545.

Mireault, G. C., Crockenberg, S. C., Sparrow, J. E., Cousineau, K., Pettinato, C., & Woodard, K. (2015). Laughing matters: Infant humor in the context of parental affect. *Journal of Experimental Child Psychology, 136,* 30–41.

Nwokah, E. E., Hsu, H.-C., Dobrowolska, O., & Fogel, A. (1994). The development of laughter in mother-infant communication: Timing parameters and temporal sequences. *Infant Behavior and Development, 17,* 23–35.

Panksepp, J., & Burgdorf, J. (2003). 'Laughing' rats and the evolutionary antecedents of human joy? *Physiology and Behavior, 79,* 533–547.

Porter, F. L., Miller, R. H., & Marshall, R. E. (1986). Neonatal pain cries: Effects of circumcision on acoustic features and perceived urgency. *Child Development, 57,* 790–802.

Preyer, W. (1889). *The mind of the child.* New York, NY: Appleton.

Protopapas, A., & Eimas, P. D. (1997). Perceptual differences in infant cries revealed by modifications of acoustic features. *Journal of the Acoustical Society of America, 102,* 3723–3734.

Reddy, V. (2003). On being the object of attention: Implications for self-other consciousness. *Trends in Cognitive Science, 7,* 397–402.

Reddy, V., & Mireault, G. (2014). Teasing and clowning in infancy. *Current Biology, 25,* R20–R23.

Reddy, V. (2019). Meeting infant affect. *Developmental Psychology, 55,* 2020–2024.

Reissland, N., Francis, B., Mason, J., & Lincoln, K. (2011). Do facial expressions develop before birth? *PLoS One, 6,* e24081.

Reissland, N., Francis, B., Aydin, E., Mason, J., & Exley, K. (2014). Development of prenatal lateralization: Evidence from fetal mouth movements. *Physiology and Behaviour, 131,* 160–163.

Ross, H. S., & Lollis, S. P. (1989). A social relations analysis of toddler peer relationships. *Child Development, 60,* 1082–1091.

Rothbart, M. (1981). Measurement of temperament in infancy. *Child Development, 52,* 569–578.

Roth-Hanania, R., Davidov, M., & Zahn-Waxler, C. (2011). Empathy development from 8 to 16 months: Early signs of concerns for others. *Infant Behavior and Development, 34*, 447–458.

Sagi, A., & Hoffman, M. L. (1976). Empathic distress in the newborn. *Developmental Psychology, 12*, 175–176.

Simner, M. L. (1971). Newborn's response to the cry of another infant. *Developmental Psychology, 5*, 136–150.

Sroufe, L. A., & Waters, E. (1976). The ontogenesis of smiling and laughing: A perspective on the organization of development in infancy. *Psychological Review, 83*, 173–189.

Washburn, R. W. (1929). A study of the smiling and laughing of infants in the first year of life. *Genetic Psychology Monographs, 6*, 403–537.

Wormann, V., Holodynski, M., Kartner, J., & Keller, H. (2012). A cross-cultural comparison of the development of the social smile: A longitudinal study of infant and maternal imitation in 6- and 12-week-old infants. *Infant Behavior and Development, 35*, 335–347.

Chapter 5

Fear and Loathing in Infancy and Childhood

As infants grow older, their expressions of distress begin to differ, depending on the situation and the specific challenges facing the infants. In addition to fussing and crying when experiencing discomfort, infants communicate how they feel with distinct facial expressions. Two of the earliest facial expressions emerging in infancy are disgust and fear, both being negative reactions to people or things within infants' surroundings. Expressions of disgust are immediate; infants encounter smells or tastes that they dislike and show how they feel about them. Expressions of fear may also be immediate, when the infants encounter an alarming object or situation and become distressed immediately, but they may also experience fear in anticipation of strange or intimidating situations. Anticipatory fears develop as children grow older and retain memories of people, things, or places that have frightened them in the past. Both disgust and fear can be seen as emotions that impel children to escape or avoid people or situations that may harm them.

Feeling fearful in unfamiliar or threatening environments is a universal human experience that has been studied by psychologists since the 19th century (Hall, 1897). Being capable of feeling fear is adaptive, an emotional response to strangeness or novelty that may signal potential danger. The extent to which we feel fear is often related to our lack of power to control what is happening in our surroundings. The inability to control what's happening around us is already observable in infancy.

Infants' Fears

Fear is an emotional state in which we anticipate distressing or dangerous experiences. For example, feeling afraid of the dark is not just a visual reaction to the absence of light. Rather, when we cannot see where we're going and what we might find there, we may feel fearful of what could happen to us. In other words, we are anticipating possible unpleasant

DOI: 10.4324/9781003483793-7

things that we might encounter. Different fears emerge over the course of infancy.

Looming Objects

Looming Objects

A visual experience in which visual stimuli, such as moving dots or pictures of objects, appear to be moving toward a participant's face.

One of the first signs of fear is infants' reactions to looming objects, visual displays that appear to be heading right toward the infants' faces. These displays have been used to measure infants' depth perception (e.g., Vagnoni, Lourenco, & Longo, 2012). The experimenters were of course not actually flinging objects at infants, but rather showing them patterns of moving dots or pictures of objects that are growing larger and thus seem to be heading straight for the infants' faces. Conversely, pictures of objects that seem to be growing smaller are seen as moving away.

The infants' reactions to the moving dots depend on the development of their depth perception over time. One- or two-month-old infants watch the dots but do not react defensively; four- to six-month-olds blink; adults flinch (Yonas et al., 1977; Kayed & van der Meer, 2000). Neuroimaging has shown that people's reactions to looming objects are supported by the visual system, in particular the superior colliculus, but there is also an emotional component to the experience (Thieu, Ayzenberg, Lourenco, & Kragel, 2024). Even adults will perceive pictures of threatening objects moving toward them as more frightening than more anodyne objects (McGuire, Ciersdorff, Gillath, & Vitevich, 2021).

Fear of Falling

After they learn to crawl, infants begin to explore their homes and other places, and they start to be sensitive to potential danger in their environments. Fear of heights emerges when infants who can move around on their own have also developed depth perception, which has been tested using a piece of equipment known as the 'visual cliff' (Gibson & Walk, 1960). A strong piece of plexiglass is laid across two compartments of a large rectangular box. Material with a checkerboard pattern is placed beneath the plexiglass surface in both compartments. In one compartment, the checkerboard material is placed right under the glass surface; in the other compartment, it is placed at the bottom of the box. Although the glass surface supports the infant's weight across both compartments, it looks as though there is a drop-off point where the infant might fall into the second compartment...a visual but not a physical cliff. In the initial study of infants' reactions to the visual cliff, infants crawled across the checkerboard surface but avoided the apparent drop-off (Gibson & Walk, 1960).

This finding implied that infants have an innate fear of heights; however, subsequent studies have questioned that assumption. In one study, those infants who could not yet or had recently started to locomote around their environments were less likely to avoid the visual cliff; they were somewhat likely to fling themselves off the whole apparatus (Kretch & Adolph, 2013). With age and more experience moving around the world, infants learn to judge heights and avoid apparent drop-offs (Campos, Bertenthal, and Kermoian, 1992).

Visual Cliff

An apparatus with a plexiglass top that covers two adjoining boxes, one with a visual pattern right underneath the top and the other with the same pattern on the floor. This makes it look as though there is a drop from one side of the apparatus to the other. Infants are encouraged by their parents to crawl across the top of the apparatus. The visual cliff was not only designed to measure infants' depth perception, but it is also used in studies of infants' fears and their trust in their parents.

Wariness with Unfamiliar People

As infants grow older and become emotionally attached to their parents and other caregivers, they may grow wary of unfamiliar people, a behaviour which some psychologists have labelled 'fear of strangers' (e.g., Sroufe, 1977). Infants' wariness of unfamiliar people is seen soon after they become able to

Wariness

Signs of children's negative reactions and avoidance of people, things, and situations without overt expressions of fear and distress.

move around their environments by crawling or learning to walk (Brand, Escobar, & Patrick, 2020). However, the degree of fearful behaviour is influenced by the extent to which infants have control over the situation and the way the unfamiliar people behave, for example, whether they approach the infants or sit and wait for the infants to decide whether or not to come to them (Ross & Goldman, 1977). Fearful reactions may increase as the infants approach their first birthdays, but there are considerable individual differences in infants' reactions to unfamiliar people (Braungart-Rieker, Hill-Soderland, & Karrass, 2010).

Some strangers are definitely more intimidating than others. For example, during a simulated birthday party in a playroom, 12-month-old infants and their caregivers were joined by two unfamiliar companions, a woman dressed as a fairy tale princess and a human-sized teddy bear (Hay et al., 2017). Of the 250 infants who were observed at the birthday parties, only 5% became distressed by the fairy tale princess, with another 5% showing some signs of wariness. Unsurprisingly, 20% became distressed upon meeting the bear, with another 5% showing some wariness.

However, the majority of the infants showed neutral or positive emotion during the birthday parties. This suggests not only that there are individual differences in responding to strangers, but also that the infants are judging some strangers to be more worrying than others. In general, the more intrusive the stranger is, the less likely the infants will respond positively.

Fear of Being Left Behind

As infants develop the abilities to move on their own volition, first rolling or crawling and then learning to walk, they move away from their caregivers to explore their surroundings. As they do so, they express interest and amusement, often laughing, smiling and looking back to share their new experiences with their caregivers. Their emotions change when their caregivers move away from them: they may fuss or cry and, if mobile, follow their companions. Thus, infants may willingly explore a new environment but show fear of being separated from the adults who are looking after them when it is the adults themselves who are walking away.

> **Strange Situation**
>
> An experimental procedure in attachment research that consists of a series of three-minute episodes in which infants meet unfamiliar people and are briefly left alone without their parents. Their reactions are classified into different attachment styles.

Infants' responses to unfamiliar people and to separation from their primary caregivers have been studied in depth, using a paradigm known as the 'Strange Situation' that was developed by psychologists conducting research on infants' attachment to their parents (Ainsworth, 1969; Ainsworth, Blehar, Waters, & Wall, 2015; Bowlby, 1969). The Strange Situation is a standardized procedure in which a parent and infant visit a playroom where they are observed. In the course of the Strange Situation, which takes less than 15 minutes, infants enter a strange environment, meet a friendly stranger and cope with being left alone when the parent goes out of the room. Different infants react to this procedure in different ways, ranging from indifference to extreme upset. In general, meeting a stranger provokes less distress than the separation from the parent (Ainsworth et al., 2015), which suggests that being left behind in an unfamiliar environment is highly fear-provoking.

Ainsworth and her colleagues focused on individual differences and identified distinct profiles of infants' responses to the Strange Situation, which they examined as different types of attachment relationships. Initially, Ainsworth compared three different patterns of infants' behaviour:

> Pattern A babies tended to maintain exploration across all episodes, not to be upset by separations from the mother, and to avoid her when reunited with her. Pattern C babies tended to be wary of the stranger, intensely upset by the separations and ambivalent to the mother when she returned, both wanting to be close to her and at the same time being angry with her, thus being difficult to soothe. Pattern B babies, on the other hand, were ready to explore when the mother was present, less so when she was absent and prompt to seek to be close to the mother in the reunion episodes or at least to initiate positive interaction with her across a distance, showing neither the avoidance nor the angry resistance shown by the other two groups.
>
> (Ainsworth, 1985, p. 775–776)

These three types of attachment relationships were defined partly on the basis of the degree of fear in response to unfamiliar people and being separated from the mother, as well as the extent to which the infants sought comfort in the mother's presence. In later work, Ainsworth's colleagues identified a fourth pattern, 'Disorganized Attachment' (Main & Solomon, 1986). Attachment relationships that are labelled as disorganized are complex and contradictory and may show fear of the parent as well as the stranger (Duchinsky & Solomon, 2017).

Fear in Middle Childhood

What Are School-Aged Children Most Afraid of?

As children grow older, they often develop specific fears. Being afraid of certain things is very common in the middle childhood years. For example, in a representative sample of families living in the UK at the beginning of the 21st century (Meltzer, Vostanis, Dogra Doos, Ford, & Goodman, 2009), parents were asked if their children were afraid of the following things: animals; injuries, blood, or injections; the dark; dentists or doctors; thunderstorms; heights; being ill; supernatural beings; loud noises; costumed characters; enclosed spaces; strange bathrooms; or particular types of transport (e.g., trains, aeroplanes, and buses). About a third of the children in that sample were reported to have at least one of those fears. Their most common fears were blood, injections, and the dark. Other work has similarly found that many children are also afraid of heights and animals (Ollendick, King, & Muris, 2002). Some fears are clearly more common than others, although that depends partly on a child's age and the cultural context in which that child is growing up.

Children often feel fear for other people, not just for themselves. For example, in a study of children's emotional reactions to the Covid pandemic, some Swedish children reported that they were afraid they might infect their grandparents if they became infected themselves, as the illness might be more dangerous for older people (Sarkadi, Torp, Perez-Andersson, & Warner, 2021).

Playing around with Fear

Children often test their own levels of fear in the context of play. It is notable that when children are playing with other children, they often challenge themselves to explore new places or do new things, such as riding a roller coaster or climbing up a tree. When playing a game of hide-and-seek, one of the children is pretending to be lost; when climbing up a slide or swinging in the air, children are challenging themselves to face heights without fear. For example, in a combined observational and qualitative interview study of preschool children in Norway, six categories of 'risky play' were identified: '(1) play with great heights; (2) play with high speed; (3) play with harmful tools; (4) play near dangerous elements; (5) rough-and-tumble play; and (6) play where the children can "disappear"/get lost' (Hansen Sandseter, 2007).

Traditional entertainments for children, such as going to an amusement park or a circus, similarly introduce them to situations that could be frightening but might also be quite fun. These childhood entertainments can be seen as cultural ways of fostering children's abilities to engage with potentially frightening experiences in safe spaces and come away from those experiences having been entertained. Playgrounds, amusement parks, and circuses have been designed to give children the chance to meet their fears in a safe environment and learn how to manage their emotional reactions. Nonetheless, while some children may enjoy these traditional entertainments, others may find them emotionally challenging. Such individual differences in response to challenging experiences begin to emerge in infancy.

Disgust

Signs of Distaste and Disgust

Infants' interest in people and things propels them to explore their worlds. When they do so, they may soon smell or taste quite unpleasant things.

Other unpleasant things—like sour or bitter tastes—may be offered to them by their parents or other caregivers as they transition away from breastfeeding to eating solids. In response to these new food challenges, infants are likely to express disgust. Indeed, the first definition of disgust in the *Oxford English Dictionary* refers to food: 'Strong distaste or disrelish for food in general, or for any particular kind or dish of food,' which precedes the more general definition 'Strong repugnance, aversion, or repulsion, excited by that which is loathsome or offensive' (p. 750).

However, the experience of disgust goes beyond bad tastes:

> Disgust can be defined as an emotional reaction that activates the parasympathetic nervous system, generates feelings of nausea and a characteristic facial expression, and results in the behavioural avoidance of a stimulus. This is importantly different from distaste, which is a phylogenetically ancient sensory response to toxins that requires gustatory contact.
>
> (Rottman, 2014)

Disgust is thought by some to be a uniquely human emotion (Kelly, 2011; Rozin et al., 2008), potentially because it is cognitively complex, or perhaps because humans encountered new survival pressures when their diets become more omnivorous or when they began living in dense groups. Although the experience of disgust goes beyond food preferences, the first facial signs of disgust in infants are displayed when the infants are offered bitter or sour tastes that they dislike. The biological infrastructure for infants' sense of taste begins to develop even before they are born, with taste buds emerging in the first two months of gestation (Forestell & Mennella, 2017). Infants are born with the abilities to taste and judge their food.

When adults confront something that they find disgusting, they often wrinkle their noses and raise their upper lips (Ekman & Friesen, 1978). Such expressions are not so clearly observed in infants (Oaten, Stevenson, & Case, 2009), who may simply start to cry or shrink back from the disgusting objects or situations. However, even newborns' facial expressions do communicate positive or negative reactions to different experiences. For example, when tasting sweet liquids, infants show signs of contentment, as opposed to wrinkling their noses and grimacing in response to sour and bitter tastes (Rosenstein & Oster, 1988). Subsequent work has shown that infants may also respond positively to umami tastes such as soup broth (Forestell & Mennella, 2017).

Children continue to express disgust at certain tastes and smells as they grow older. For example, in one study that examined video records of family meals, children expressed disgust at least once per hour (Wiggins, 2013). However, older children's feelings of disgust go beyond their food preferences. Parents' reports of the things and experiences that their children find distasteful or disgusting revealed three main categories of disgusting objects or events (Stevenson, Oaten, Case, Repacholi, & Wagland, 2010): 'lack of hygiene' (e.g., eating with dirty hands, spitting on the sidewalk, and strong-smelling flatulence); 'exposure to death' (e.g., encountering a dead cat or a dead bird); and 'unusual and unpleasant sights,' such as seeing maggots in the rubbish bin or a human hand inside a jar.

Such sights or smells signal the possibility of contamination, illness, and possible death. Children might learn about contamination dangers from their parents, but some evolutionary theorists argue that disgust responses are innate, that they have survival value and have been selected for in human evolution (e.g., Rozin, Haidt, & McCauley, 2008). However, children may also learn to be disgusted by things that could injure them or make them ill, as taught by their parents (Sullivan & Lewis, 2003).

Moral Disgust

In later childhood, children may sometimes experience 'moral disgust' when other people violate social or moral norms. In a study of six-, seven-, and nine-year-olds (Danovitch & Bloom, 2009), children were asked to say whether or not a hypothetical person's actions could be called disgusting; a control set of actions was also provided. Some of the actions described to the children were physical (e.g., people putting their hands in slime), whereas others were sociomoral (e.g., stealing money from a child or telling mean lies about a friend). The children sometimes judged the immoral acts as disgusting (verbally or by pointing to photographs of an adult's 'disgust face'), but they did so less than when confronted with examples of physically disgusting acts. Some children also respond to immoral actions with anger rather than disgust (Azner, Tenenbaum, & Russell, 2023).

Temperament

Individual patterns of reactions to familiar and unfamiliar situations; for example, different reactions to potentially fearful situations are seen as a component of an individual's underlying temperament.

Infants' Individual Temperaments

Different infants react to their worlds in different ways; they have different temperaments. The initial studies of infants' temperament explored individual differences in several dimensions, including activity level, positive affect (smiling and laughing), and what has been termed 'distress to limitations,' when infants' behaviour is restricted in some way, often for their own safety (e.g., Rothbert, 1981). Those studies revealed individual differences across several different dimensions, such as high versus low activity level and high versus low fearfulness. Other studies of temperament have called attention to different types of temperament, for example, children who are classified as over-controlled, under-controlled, and resilient (Robins et al., 1996). One such study classified children as being typical, expressive, or fearful (van den Akker, et al., 2010). Thus, in different classification systems, fearfulness is identified as a key dimension of temperament.

Fear is a primary emotion, but different infants experience different levels of fearfulness when they are presented with new people and unfamiliar places. When confronted with a new place or a stranger, some infants freeze up or start to cry. Other infants plunge into such situations immediately, engaging with their new acquaintances and showing few signs of fear. These differences in children's fearful as opposed to fearless temperament persist as children grow older and have an impact on the choices that they make, whether they seek comfort in familiar people and things or enjoy exploring unknown people and places in their social worlds. Such studies of infant temperament suggest that individual differences in these emotions emerge in the first year of life. In some cases, as we shall see in the next chapter, children's disgust reactions and fearfulness may develop into clinically significant phobias and anxiety disorders.

Further Reading

Cowie, H. (2020). The impact of the COVID-19 on the mental health and well-being of children and young people. *Children and Society*, *35*, 62–74.

Cresswell, C., & Willetts, L. (2019). *Helping your child with fears and worries*. London: Robinson.

Rothbart, M. K. (2011). *Becoming who we are: Temperament and personality in development*. London: Guilford.

References

Ainsworth, M. D. S. (1969). Object relations, dependency, and attachment: A theoretical review of the infant-mother relationship. *Child Development*, *40*, 969–1025.

Ainsworth, M. D. S. (1985). Patterns of infant-mother attachments. *Bulletin of the New York Academy of Medicine*, *61*, 775–776.

Ainsworth, M. D. S., Blehar, M., Waters, E., & Wall, S. (2015). *Patterns of attachment: A psychological study of the strange situation*. New York, NY: Psychology Press.

Azner, A., Tenenbaum, H. R., & Russell, P. S. (2023). Is moral disgust socially learned? *Emotion*, *23*, 289–301.

Bowlby, J. (1960). Separation anxiety. *International Journal of Psychoanalysis, 41,* 89–113.

Brand, R. J., Escobar, K., & Patrick, A. M. (2020). Coincidence or cascade? The temporal relation between locomotor behaviors and the emergence of stranger anxiety. *Infant Behavior and Development, 58,* 101423.

Braungart-Rieker, J. M., Hill-Soderland, A. L., & Karrass, J. (2010). Fear and anger: Reactivity trajectories from 4 to 16 months: The roles of temperament, regulation, and maternal sensitivity. *Developmental Psychology, 46,* 791–804.

Campos, J. J., Bertenthal, B. I., & Kermoian, R. (1992). Early experience and emotional development: The emergence of wariness of heights. *Psychological Science, 3,* 61–64.

Danovitch, J., & Bloom, P. (2009). Children's extension of disgust to physical and moral events. *Emotion, 9,* 107–112.

Duchinsky, R., & Solomon, J. (2017). Infant disorganized attachment: Clarifying levels of analysis. *Clinical Child Psychology and Psychiatry, 22,* 524–538.

Ekman, P., & Friesen, W. V. (1978). Facial action coding system (FACS). Environmental Psychology and Nonverbal Behav. APA PsychTests.

Forestell, C. A., & Mennella, J. A. (2017). The relationship between infant facial expressions and food acceptance. *Current Nutrition Reports, 6,* 141–147.

Gibson, E. J., & Walk, R. D. (1960). The 'visual cliff.' *Scientific American, 202,* 64–71.

Hall, G. S. (1897). A study of fears. *The American Journal of Psychology, 8,* 147–249.

Hansen Sandsteter, E. B. (2007). Categorising risky play: How can we identify risk-taking in children's play? *European Early Childhood Education Research Journal, 15,* 237–252.

Hay, D. F., van Goozen, S., Mundy, L., Phillips, R., Roberts, S., Meeuwsen, M., Goodyer, I., & Perra, O. (2017). If you go down to the woods today: Infants' distress during a Teddy Bear's Picnic in ration to peer relations and later emotional problems. *Infancy, 22,* 552–570.

Kayed, N. S., & van der Meer, A. (2000). Timing strategies used in defensive blinking to optical collisions in 5- to 7-month-old infants. *Infant Behavior and Development, 23,* 253–270.

Kelly, D. (2011). *Yuck! The nature and moral significance of disgust.* Cambridge, MA: MIT Press.

Kretch, K. S., & Adolph, K. (2013). Cliff or step? Posture-related learning at the edge of a drop-off. *Child Development, 84,* 226–240.

Main, M., & Solomon, J. (1986). Discovery of an insecure-disorganized/disoriented attachment pattern. In T. B. Brazelton & M. W. Yogman (Eds.), *Affective development in infancy* (pp. 95–124). Norwood, NJ: Ablex.

McGuire, A., Ciersdorff, A., Gillath, O., & Vitevitch, M. (2021). Effect of cognitive load and type of object on the visual looming bias. *Attention, Perception, and Psychophysics, 83,* 1508–1517.

Meltzer, H., Vostanis, P., Dogra, N., Doos, L., Ford, T., & Goodman, R. (2009). Children's specific fears. *Child: Care, Health, and Development, 35,* 781–789.

Oaten, M., Stevenson, R. J., & Case, T. L. (2009). Disgust as a disease-avoidant mechanism. *Psychological Bulletin, 135,* 303–321.

Ollendick, T. H., King, N. J., & Muris, P. (2002). Fears and phobias in children: Phenomenology, epidemiology, and aetiology. *Child and Adolescent Mental Health*, 7, 98–106.

Robins, R. W., John, O. P., Caspi, A., Moffitt, T. E., & Stouthamer-Loeber, M. (1996). Resilient, overcontrolled, and undercontrolled boys: Three replicable personality types. *Journal of Personality and Social Psychology*, 70, 157–171.

Rosenstein, D., & Oster, H. (1988). Differential facial responses to four basic tastes in newborns. *Child Development*, 59, 1555–1568.

Ross, H. S. & Goldman, B. D. (1977). Establishing new social relations in infancy. In T. Alloway, P. Pliner, & L. Krames (Eds.), *Attachment behaviour*. New York, NY: Springer.

Rothbert, M. (1981). Measurement of temperament in infancy. *Child Development*, 52, 569–578.

Rottman, J. (2014). Evolution, development, and the emergence of disgust. *Evolutionary Psychology*, 12, 417–433.

Rozin, P., Haidt, J., & McCauley, C. R. (2008). *Disgust*. New York: Guilford Press.

Sarkadi, A., Torp, L. S., Pérez-Andersson, A., & Warner, G. (2021). Children's expressions of worry during the Covid-19 pandemic in Sweden. *Journal of Pediatric Psychology*, 46, 939–949.

Sroufe, L. A. (1977). Wariness of strangers and the study of infant development. *Child Development*, 48, 731–746.

Stevenson, R. J., Oaten, M. J., Case, T. I., Repacholi, B. M., & Wagland, P. (2010). Children's response to adult disgust elicitors: Development and acquisition. *Developmental Psychology*, 46, 165–177.

Sullivan, M. W., & Lewis, M. (2003). Emotional expressions of young infants and children: A practitioner's primer. *Infants and Young Children*, 16, 120–142.

Thieu, M. K., Ayzenberg, V., Lourenco, S. F., & Kragel, P. A. (2024). Visual looming is a primitive for human emotion. *iScience*, 27, 6.

Vagnoni, E., Lourenco, S. F., & Longo, M. R. (2012). Threat modulates perception of looming visual stimuli. *Current Biology*, 22, PR826–R827.

van den Akker, A. L., Dekovic, M., Prinzie, P., & Asscher, J. J. (2010). Toddlers' temperament profiles: Stability and relations to negative and positive parenting. *Journal of Abnormal Child Psychology*, 38, 485–495.

Wiggins, S. (2013). The social life of 'eugh': Disgust as assessment in family mealtimes. *British Journal of Social Psychology*, 52, 489–509.

Yonas, A., Bechtold, G., Frankel, D., Gordon, F. R., McRoberts, G., Norcia, A., & Sternfeld, S. (1977). Development of sensitivity to information for impending collision. *Attention, Perception, and Psychophysics*, 21, 97–104.

Chapter 6

Worries, Phobias, and Anxiety Disorders

As we have seen in the foregoing chapter, some children are more fearful than others. Other children only rarely feel fear. Both extreme fearfulness and extreme fearlessness are associated with other mental health problems. In this chapter, we focus on psychological issues associated with more extreme fears and worries.

Children's Worries

It is not uncommon for children to worry, often about their immediate futures: Will it rain tomorrow and, if so, will we have to cancel the picnic? Will there be a surprise quiz in maths class? Some worries may be long-standing: Am I ever going to grow taller? Will Dad ever come home again? Worrying combines guessing about the future with an emotional disquiet that verges on fear. Indeed, when we worry, we are often considering whether or not frightening or otherwise unpleasant things will happen to us in the future.

Different children worry about different things, and what they worry about depends on their age as well as their individual circumstances. For example, in a study in which 4- to 12-year-old Dutch children were interviewed about their fears, worries, and frightening dreams (Muris, Merkelbach, Gadet, & Mourlaet, 2000), 74% of girls and 61% of boys reported that they worried about various things, with their personal harm, their parents' or grandparents' deaths, separation from their parents, and doing poorly on tests being the most worrisome. Worrying was more common for the older children. In particular, the older children were more worried about their test performance, while the youngest children were most worried about separation from their parents.

When parents worry, their children may be worrying as well. Children's worries are also affected by family circumstances that affect their parents. However, children also worry about events that are affecting the world beyond their homes. For example, in Sweden during the height of the

DOI: 10.4324/9781003483793-8

Covid epidemic, 1,047 children and 550 adolescents responded to an anonymous web-based survey that asked four open-ended questions, one of which was 'Is there anything you are worried about when it comes to Corona?' (Sarkadi, Sahlin Torp, Perez-Andersson, & Warner, 2021). In response to that question, 77% of the respondents reported worrying. There were no significant age differences. One 5-year-old worried, 'that we children are left alone when old people die. But Mum says we will not be' (p. 943). A 14-year-old confided, 'I worry it will wipe out the whole world' (p. 944). But, in that sample, some of the adolescents were also concerned about their own future after the pandemic subsided. They worried about whether missing out on school and usual teenage activities would have a negative effect on their future lives.

The Emergence of Anxiety Disorders in Childhood

As we have seen, individual differences in fearfulness are already evident in infancy. Some children may become less fearful over time, but for a minority of children, their fears and worries become incessant, dominating their daily lives and making it difficult for them to make friends, feel comfortable in school, and deal with new challenges. In such cases, early fearfulness may develop into clinically significant anxiety. This may happen quite early in development. On average, anxiety disorders first emerge when a child is six years old (Strawn, Lu, Peris, Levine, & Walkup, 2021). Specific fears are typically the first disorder to emerge by age six.

The definitions of anxiety disorders used in medical classification systems such as the International Classification of Diseases (ICD) and the Diagnostic and Statistical Manual (DSM) are often used to identify the children who might need help from clinical psychologists or child psychiatrists (see Table 4.1). Using one or the other of these diagnostic systems, interviewers ask questions about the child's reactions to unfamiliar people and various situations that might provoke fear or distress. The findings from these interviews are then analysed to identify how many of the children being studied are experiencing high levels of fear or anxiety symptoms.

For example, in a nationally representative study of children and adolescents in Northern Ireland, teenagers between 11 and 19 years old completed questionnaires about their own mental health, in particular anxiety disorders and depression; in the case of younger children, parents completed equivalent questionnaires about their children's mental health. Their reports revealed that overall, about 11% of the young people were experiencing some of these mental health problems, although the highest rate of problems was reported by the older adolescents (16- to

19-year-olds), 19% of whom reported experiencing symptoms of anxiety and/or depression. About 12% of younger teenagers reported such problems; similarly, 12% of the parents of five- to ten-year-olds reported that their children were showing symptoms of anxiety or depression.

More precise details about children's experience of anxiety over time can be provided by longitudinal studies that include interviews and questionnaires about children's and teenagers' mental health. In many such studies, the participants are recruited from nationally or regionally representative samples where the participants or their parents can be interviewed about their mental health at different ages. For example, in a large, long-running study of children who had been born in or near the city of Bristol, UK, parents completed questionnaires when their children were 8, 10, and 13 years old (Morales-Munoz, Hett, Hempston, Mallikarjun, & Marwaha, 2022). Between 2% and 3% of the children met the ICD diagnostic criteria for an anxiety disorder. At 8 and 13 years, specific fears and general anxiety were the most common subtypes of anxiety reported; however, at 10 years of age, fear-related anxiety was the most common subtype. This type of anxiety can also be seen much earlier in the child's life.

Specific Phobias

Specific Phobias

Extreme fears of particular objects or experiences, such as fear of heights or fear of the dark.

Phobias

Phobias have the following markers: they are 'out of proportion to the demands of the situation'; they 'cannot be explained or reasoned away'; are 'beyond voluntary control'; and 'lead to the avoidance of the feared situation'

The first type of anxiety disorder to appear in childhood, specific phobias, begins around six years of age. Specific phobias are the most common type of anxiety disorder in childhood and adolescence, with approximately one in five young people experiencing such phobias (Bennett et al., 2015).

Fear is a basic emotion that most people feel from time to time, in certain situations. Many things and situations might occasionally make us feel afraid. Some fearfulness is adaptive, in that it alerts us to possible dangers. However, some people experience strong fear of specific things or situations, which can actually interfere with their ability to explore and enjoy their worlds. Such focused fears are termed specific phobias. In contrast to ordinary fears, phobias have the following markers: they are 'out of proportion to the demands of the situation'; they 'cannot be explained or reasoned away'; are 'beyond voluntary control'; and 'lead to the avoidance of the feared situation' (Marks, 1987; quoted in Ollendick, King, & Muris, 2002).

Children's specific fears were already being studied nearly 100 years ago, when 400 children were interviewed about the things they were afraid of, which included physical dangers and supernatural beings (Jersild, Markey, & Jersild, 1933). Decades later, children were still reporting their fears of ghosts and monsters but were also afraid of being injured, being put in danger, or becoming victims of war (Bauer, 1976; Croake, 1969).

The types of things that frighten children endure into this century. In a systematic review of specific phobias, children as well as adults reported being afraid of animals, heights, water, and stormy weather, as well as flying in aeroplanes (LeBeau, Liao, Wittchen, Beesdo-Baum, Ollendick, & Craske, 2010). About half the people in that study who had a specific phobia were either afraid of heights or animals. Animal phobias, in particular, emerged in early childhood.

Separation Anxiety

Separation anxiety is another type of anxiety disorder that originates relatively early in childhood, when some young children experience extreme fears and worries about being separated from their parents or other caregivers. Separation anxiety disorder (SAD), which on average emerges by seven years of age (Strawn et al., 2021). However, children's reactions to separation

> **Separation Anxiety**
>
> An anxiety disorder that originates relatively early in childhood, when some young children experience extreme fears and worries about being separated from their parents or other caregivers.

from their parents has been a key concept in psychoanalytic theory that has influenced later attachment theory, beginning with John Bowlby's observations of children who had been separated from their parents when they were hospitalized, the usual practice in the mid-20th century (Bowlby, 1960). Bowlby argued that the children in hospitals would be cared for by any number of nurses (often student nurses) on different shifts, so they would not be able to establish any relationships with particular nurses whom they saw regularly. The hospitalized children might see their mothers briefly but, in some cases, not at all. Bowlby proposed that what the children in hospitals were experiencing was a progression from protest to despair to detachment. Bowlby's and others' studies of the effect of hospitalization on children's relationships with their parents eventually led to changes in hospital practice. However, children's separation anxiety may also be seen in other circumstances, such as going to school for the first time.

Some degree of distress when infants are separated from their parents is quite common. However, as children grow older and become used to spending time with other people, in playgroups or nursery schools, only a minority of children still experience extreme distress when separated from their parents. For example, in a very large sample of nearly 30,000 Iranian children and teenagers, 5% experienced clinically defined separation anxiety (Mohammadi, Baderfam, Khalegi, Hooshyari, Ahmadi, & Zandifar, 2020). In that sample, girls and boys were equally likely to experience separation anxiety.

Separation anxiety may increase when young children are making transitions from home to school or from one school to another. For example, in a representative sample of over 3000 children born in Trondheim, Norway, separation anxiety increased when children made the transition from preschool to primary school (Steinsbekk, Ranum, & Wickstrom, 2022). As in the Iranian sample, there were no significant associations with gender differences: 1% of girls and 3% of boys were diagnosed with separation anxiety.

Social Anxiety

Social Anxiety

People's experiences of extreme discomfort in social situations, particularly when interacting with individuals whom they have just met or know only slightly.

As children grow older, they may experience extreme discomfort in social situations. Shy children who, as infants, had shown behavioural inhibition when encountering a novel situation or meeting unfamiliar people might find it increasingly difficult to deal with social situations in their teenage years. One survey suggested that about one in ten teenagers (11% of girls and 7% of boys) found social situations very difficult to deal with, worrying about embarrassing themselves and being teased or rejected by their peers (Merikangas, 2010).

A more recent study surveyed 6825 teenagers and young adults in seven countries (Brazil, China, Indonesia, Russia, Thailand, the United States, and Vietnam). The investigators found that 30% of the teenagers reported that they were experiencing the diagnostic symptoms of social anxiety (Jeffries & Ungar, 2020). The prevalence of social anxiety was somewhat higher in the young adults. Shyness and behavioural inhibition in childhood are predictors of later social anxiety. In a meta-analysis of studies in which young children had been observed showing behavioural inhibition in response to novel situations, those children were subsequently almost six times more likely to meet the criteria for social anxiety at later ages (OR = 5.89; Sandstrom, Uher, & Pavlova, 2020).

General Anxiety Disorder and Panic Disorder

As its name suggests, General Anxiety Disorder (GAD) is more diffuse than separation anxiety or social anxiety, with a range of physical symptoms that indicate a child or teenager's general emotional discomfort. These symptoms, which include insomnia, fatigue, and muscle tension, as well as difficulties in concentrating and general irritability (Crawley et al., 2014), are seen in about 2% of adolescents (Merikangas et al., 2010). Panic disorder emerges in early adolescence and increases over the teenage years. Panic attacks, which feature both physical and cognitive symptoms, are sudden episodes of fear, which can occur unexpectedly, 'out of the blue,' but can also be triggered by particular events (Strawn et al., 2021).

Panic Attacks

Experiences of sudden episodes of fear, which can occur unexpectedly, without warning. Panic attacks feature both physical and cognitive symptoms, are sudden episodes of fear, which can occur unexpectedly, 'out of the blue,' but can also be triggered by particular events.

Risk Factors for Anxiety Disorders

Which children are most likely to be affected by anxiety disorders? It should be noted that childhood anxiety is relatively common. For example, in a community sample of seven-year-olds that was demographically representative of the entire UK population (Hay et al., 2021), 50% of children met the general diagnostic criteria for anxiety symptoms, as reported by the children's parents. Those data were collected prior to the Covid-19 pandemic, which further affected children's emotional health. This suggests that anxiety is relatively common; factors in the child, family, and broader environment influence a child's chance of experiencing an anxiety disorder (Strawn et al., 2021).

Gene-environment Correlation

A concept that proposes that a person's choice of environment is associated with genetic factors. Individuals with particular genetic profiles may seek out and/ or fare better in certain environments.

Molecular Genetics

The scientific study of the structure and functions of genes at the molecular level.

Genetic Variants

Natural differences in the sequences of DNA for different individuals. These are patterns of people's individuality at the molecular level.

Anxiety may be passed on from parents to their children via both genetic and environmental pathways. Parents who are themselves anxious, including those who have been formally diagnosed with anxiety disorders, are more likely than other parents to have anxious children. In such cases, children's likelihood of developing anxiety disorders may be influenced by *gene–environment correlation* (e.g., where parents with a history of anxiety may create home environments in which children are encouraged to be cautious and apprehensive of new experiences). Molecular genetic studies are beginning to identify genetic variants associated with symptoms of anxiety (e.g., Ask, Cheesman, Jami, Levey, Purves, & Weber, 2021). Eventually this type of information about genetic factors can be lined up with information about anxiety-prone parents' caregiving environments, their anxiety about being a parent as well as their parenting practices, and their children's emerging signs of anxiety symptoms and disorders.

Further Reading

Cowie, H. (2020). The impact of COVID-19 on the mental health and well-being of children and young people. *Children and Society, 35,* 62–74.

Cresswell, C., & Willetts, L. (2019). *Helping your child with fears and worries.* London: Robinson.

Fox, N. A., Zeytinoglu, S., Valadez, E. A., Buzzell, G. A., Morales, S., & Henderson, H. A. (2022). Annual research review: Developmental pathways linking early behavioural inhibition to later anxiety. *Journal of Child Psychology and Psychiatry, 64,* 537–561.

References

Ask, H., Cheesman, S., Jami, E. S., Levey, D. F., Purves, K. L., & Weber, H. (2021). Genetic contributions to anxiety disorders: Where we are and where we are heading. *Psychological Medicine, 51,* 2231–2246.

Bauer, D. H. (1976). An exploratory study of developmental changes in children's fears *Journal of Child Psychology and Psychiatry, 17,* 69–74.

Bennett, K., Mannasis, K., Duda, S., Bagnell, A., Bernstein, G. A., Garland, E. J., Thabane, L., & Wilansky, P. (2015). Preventing child and adolescent anxiety disorders: Overview of systematic reviews. *Depression and Anxiety, 32,* 909–918.

Bowlby, J. (1960). Separation anxiety. *International Journal of Psychoanalysis*, *41*, 89–113.

Crawley, S. A., Caporino, N. E., Birmaher, B., Ginsburg, G., Piacentini, J., Albano, A. M., Sherill, J., Sakolsky, D., Compton, S. N., Rynn, M., McCracken, J., Gosch, E., Keeten, C., March, J., Walkup, J. T., & Kendall, P. C. (2014). Somatic complaints in anxious youth. *Child Psychiatry and Human Development*, *45*, 398–407.

Croake, J. W. (1969). Fears of children. *Human Development*, *12*, 239–247.

Hay, D. F., Paine, A. L., Perra, O., Cook, K. V., Hashmi, S., Robinson, C., Kairis, V., & Slade, R. (2021). Prosocial and aggressive behaviour: A longitudinal study. *Monographs of the Society for Research in Child Development*, *86*, Serial No. 341.

Jeffries, P., & Ungar, M. (2020). Social anxiety in young people: A prevalence study in seven countries. *PLoS One*, *15*, e0239133.

Jersild, A. T., Markey, F. V., & Jersild, C. L. (1933). Children's fears, dreams, wishes, daydreams, likes, dislikes, pleasant and unpleasant memories. *Child Development*, *12*, ix–172.

LeBeau, R. T., Glenn, D., Liao, B., Wittchen, H.-U., Beesdo-Baum, K., Ollendick, T., & Craske, M. G. (2010). Specific phobia: A review of DSM-IV specific phobia and preliminary recommendations for DSM-V. *Depression and Anxiety*, *27*(2), 148–167.

Mohammadi, M. R., Badrfam, R., Khalegi, A., Hooshyari, Z., Ahmadi, N., & Zandifar, A. (2020). Prevalence, comorbidity, and predictor of separation anxiety disorder in children and adolescents. *Psychiatric Quarterly*, *91*, 1415–1429.

Morales-Munoz, I., Mallikarjun, P. K., Chandan, J. S., Thayakaram, R., Upthegrove, R., & Marwaha, S. (2023). Impact of anxiety and depression across adolescence on Adverse outcomes in young adulthood: A UK birth cohort study. *British Journal of Psychiatry*, *222*, 212–220.

Merikangas, K. R., He, J.-P., Brody, D., Fisher, P. W., Bourdon, K., & Koretz, D. S. (2010). Prevalence and treatment of mental disorders among US children in the 2001–2004 NHANES. *Pediatrics*, *125*, 75–81.

Muris, P., Merkelbach, H., Gadet, B., & Mourlaet, V. (2000). Fears, worries, and Scary dreams in 4- to 12-year-old children: Their content, developmental pattern, and origins. *Journal of Clinical Child Psychology*, *29*, 43–52.

Ollendick, T. H., King, N. J., & Muris, P. (2002). Fears and phobias in children: Phenomenology, epidemiology, and aetiology. *Child and Adolescent Mental Health*, *7*, 98–106.

Sandstrom, A., Uher, R., & Pavlova, B. (2020). Prospective association between childhood behavioural inhibition and anxiety: A meta-analysis. *Research on Childhood and Adolescent Psychopathology*, *48*, 57–66.

Sarkadi, A., Torp, L. S., Pérez-Andersson, A., & Warner, G. (2021). Children's expressions of worry during the Covid-19 pandemic in Sweden. *Journal of Pediatric Psychology*, *46*, 939–949.

Steinsbekk, S., Ranum, B., & Wickstrom, L. (2022). Prevalence and course of anxiety disorders and symptoms from preschool to adolescence: A 6-wave community study. *Journal of Child Psychology and Psychiatry*, *63*, 527–534.

Strawn, J. R., Lu, L., Peris, T. S., Levine, A., & Walkup, J. T. (2021). Research review: Pediatric anxiety disorders—what have we learned in the last ten years? *Journal of Psychology and Psychiatry*, *62*, 114–139.

Chapter 7

Anger in Infancy and Childhood

Anger has been defined as 'a state of arousal that results from social conditions involving threat or frustration' (Averill, 1982; cited in Kerr & Schneider, 2008). It is perhaps not surprising that anger rises in the toddler years, when children are becoming mobile, exploring their environments, and resisting their parents' and other people's requests and demands. Infants' expressions of distress have differentiated into fearfulness, anger, and sadness. With their increasingly efficient locomotor skills, toddlers explore their worlds, crossing boundaries set by their parents and other caregivers, chasing the things that they want to touch and do. It is a time when children start to come into anger-fuelled conflict with parents, siblings, and peers.

As we have seen, in a classic study carried out nearly a century ago, Katherine Bridges (1932) proposed that specific emotional expressions only gradually emerge from newborn infants' general expressions of distress. She believed that anger was the first primary emotion to appear in children's emotional development, as a reaction to frustrating situations. To test this hypothesis, she observed three- to six-month-old infants in an orphanage in Montreal, Québec. Her observations of that small, selected sample suggested that infants' crying in response to frustrating situations could be distinguished from other signs of distress in different contexts.

However, other emotion theorists have disagreed with Bridges' differentiation theory. They have hypothesized that infants can express distinct primary emotions such as anger and fear right from the start. This raises the question of the age at which infants begin to express anger, not just general discomfort or distress. Studies of the early development of anger have used both observational methods and informants' reports.

Expressing Anger

Human beings have many ways of expressing their anger—facial expressions, angry gestures, sarcastic words, swearing, shouting, and physical

DOI: 10.4324/9781003483793-9

attacks. One person's display of anger may be responded to in different ways: attempts to calm down the angry person, or losing one's own temper, or escalating into verbal or physical conflict. Anger is a social emotion, often fuelled by frustration or another person's aggressive actions. One person's anger may be a trigger for extended conflict. These patterns of anger-fuelled conflict begin in the first years of life.

Signs of Anger in Infancy

Initially, infants show generalized distress, crying, perhaps flailing out at people and things. Subsequently, distress differentiates into different forms of emotional expression—fear, anxiety, anger, and sadness. Distinctive angry expressions are already observable in infancy.

Psychologists have used facial coding systems to study anger expressions in response to frustrating circumstances. In experimental studies, rather than waiting around for episodes of spontaneous anger, the investigators put infants in situations that were likely to trigger anger. For example, in one experimental study (Stenberg, Campos, & Emde, 1983), 30 seven-month-old infants and their mothers were invited to the laboratory. The infants were strapped into a highchair. The experimenter offered the infant a teething biscuit, then pulled it away. The biscuit was offered and taken back repeatedly; the infants' responses were video-recorded and coded for signs of 'an angry face' as defined in earlier studies of adults' emotions.

In that study, the coding system used to measure anger focused on particular facial expressions: vertical lines appearing between an infant's eyebrows; staring eyes; nose-wrinkling; pressing the lips firmly together; or, alternatively, opening them in a way that made them look square, which sometimes led to a shout. When the experimenter seized the biscuit, these facial movements were often seen, and the infants' faces became more flushed. The investigators concluded that this pattern of facial movements signalled anger in particular, not just general distress (Stenberg et al., 1983). However, other psychologists disagreed, suggesting that the facial signs of negative emotion could not be so easily categorized as anger as opposed to fear.

In a subsequent study, the experimenters physically restrained one-, four- and seven-month-old infants' movements, grasping the infants' forearms and pulling them together, holding the infants' arms for up to three minutes. As might be expected, the one-month-olds who were being restrained in this way became distressed but did not show the distinct pattern of facial expression that signalled anger in older children. However, a few of the four- and seven-month-olds did show signs of anger in their expressions. This suggests that distress gradually differentiates into different types of negative emotion, one of which is anger.

Informants' questionnaires corroborate the evidence from the laboratory frustration tasks, showing that early signs of anger emerge in the first year of life. For example, in a nationally representative, UK-based sample of over 300 six-month-olds, mothers, fathers, and grandparents (or other frequent caregivers) reported that about 60% of the infants sometimes or often experienced angry moods (Hay et al., 2010). These informants' reports were further validated by direct observation of the infants' reactions to a familiar but nonetheless frustrating situation, being strapped into a car seat. Those infants who were observed to be most distressed by being confined in the car seat were also more likely than other infants to hit or bite other people, as reported on the informants' questionnaires. These findings suggest that distinct expressions of anger, as opposed to sadness or fear, are evident by the midpoint of the first year of life. However, some children seem more prone to anger than others.

Individual Differences in Expressed Anger

Individual Differences in Infancy

Individual differences in expressing anger are bound up with the infant's overall temperament. Different methods have been used to measure infants' temperaments: questionnaires completed by parents, teachers, or others who know the child well; more detailed interviews with parents; and experimental challenges that children may react to in different ways. These include frustration tasks, which set up situations where children find it more difficult to meet their goals.

Along with the laboratory-based studies of children's reactions to frustrating situations, psychologists have sought evidence for links between the children's observed reactions to the experimental challenges in laboratory settings and their general temperaments. Were some infants already more prone to anger than others?

For example, in one such study of eight- to ten-month-olds, mothers and fathers filled out standardized questionnaires about their infant's temperament. In that study, the investigators also directly observed infants at home with their mothers, using a newly developed measure called the Lab-Tab, an experimental measure used to assess variation in infants' temperaments (Kochanska, Coy, Tjebkes, & Huserek, 2008). Three tasks within the Lab-Tab had been designed to measure the infants' tendencies to become angry when their movements were restricted. In one task, the mother buckled the infant into a car seat; in another, the mother gently held the infant's arm down for up to 30 seconds; and in a third, the infant was offered an attractive rattle, which the mother then took away.

In that study, infants responded somewhat differently to each of these emotional challenges. Their behaviour in the experimental setting did not always line up with the parents' reports. For example, the extent to which they were observed to show 'angry distress' in the frustration task was only mildly correlated with parents' ratings of their anger (and the mothers and fathers did not always agree with each other). These findings suggested that infants are emotionally flexible, with their tendencies to become angry showing up in some contexts but not others. However, some infants seem generally angrier than others.

Although anger is a primary emotion that all of us feel and express from time to time, individual differences in the expression of anger are already evident in the first months of life. For example, in a community study of over 300 infants, mothers, fathers, and a third person who knew the infant well reported whether the infant expressed anger, had temper tantrums, hit, or bit other people (Hay, Perra et al., 2010). The questionnaire was given twice, when the infant was 6 and 12 months of age. Individual differences in these behaviours were stable over the six-month time period; the questionnaire findings were correlated with direct observation of anger in response to frustration (being strapped into a car seat) and their use of force against other people. While most infants were capable of expressing anger, some were angrier than others. These early differences in infants' anger predicted their later anger and physical aggression (Hay, Paine et al., 2021).

Temper Tantrums

Children's expressions of anger and extreme displeasure may involve shouting, hitting, kicking, writhing on the floor, and destroying things.

Physical Aggression

Physical aggression includes hitting, kicking, or otherwise using force against another person's body.

Verbal Aggression

Verbal aggression includes the use of taunts, discriminatory remarks, or verbal abuse or hate speech against another person.

Other longitudinal studies have similarly identified individual differences in anger that emerge in infancy and persist into later childhood. For example, in a sample of over 300 adopted children (Liu et al., 2018), those nine-month-old infants who were most likely to express anger when their goals were thwarted continued to show anger over the next seven years. In that sample, those children who were still expressing higher levels of anger at four years of age were significantly more likely to show behavioural problems in middle childhood. These longitudinal studies have shown that, while anger is a universal emotion that we all experience, some individuals are more prone to anger than others, and those individual differences are already emerging in infancy.

Gender Differences

Some theorists have hypothesized that boys are generally more likely to express their anger than girls; this hypothesis draws on different arguments about gender differences set forth by biologists, learning theorists, social psychologists, and sociologists. These theorists have proposed that boys are more likely to be angry than girls, due to biologically based differences in their temperaments, different experiences in their family lives, and different expectations for men and women in their societies as a whole. However, despite these generally agreed-upon expectations, the evidence for gender differences is mixed, and the pattern appears to change with age.

It is possible that gender-related patterns of emotional expressions begin to emerge in early childhood, but gender differences in anger are not always apparent in the first years of life. For example, in a large sample of adopted infants, the infant girls were no less angry than the boys were (Liu et al., 2018). Similarly, in a longitudinal study of a Welsh community sample, informants reported that 6- and 12-month-old boys were somewhat angrier than girls were, but the trend was not statistically significant (Hay, Perra et al., 2010). These findings suggest that in infancy there are few differences between girls and boys in their capacities to feel and express anger. However, adults may respond to girls' and boys' anger in different ways.

Gender differences in feelings and expressions of anger appear to change over time. In observational studies, some gender differences in anger have been reported, but the direction of the difference changes over time. For example, in a meta-analysis of children's facial expressions of emotions across 166 studies with over 20,000 participants, ranging in age from infancy to adolescence (Chaplin & Aldao, 2013), boys were significantly more likely to express anger than girls were.

In childhood, the girls were more likely than boys to express sadness, empathy, and shame. In adolescence, however, girls were more likely to express anger. It is likely that social as well as biological influences affect children's feelings and expressions of anger over time.

Expression of Anger in Conflicts with Different People

Children are most likely to express anger when they are disagreeing about particular issues with their parents, siblings, and peers. In developmental psychology, conflict can be defined as an interaction in which at least one person resists, protests, or uses force against another person (Hay & Ross, 1982). Some conflicts feature resistance or protests but may be resolved without bursts of anger or physical aggression—in adulthood, it is certainly possible to engage in intellectual disagreements without

Conflict

A social interaction in which one person acts and at least one other person protests, resists, or retaliates against the first person's action or speech.

shouting or using force against one's companions, and even children can have disagreements that do not feature angry outbursts. However, in early childhood, conflicts with parents and peers may certainly contain those expressions of anger. Later in childhood and adolescence, conflicts may be less forceful but may feature hurtful speech and threats that have a negative impact on family and peer relationships. Thus, conflicts at all ages may feature expressions of anger.

Parent–Child Conflict

Acts of resistance. In the first years of life, infants and toddlers often resist things demanded of them, such as being strapped into a car seat or being given a spoonful of food that they find unpalatable. Everyday parent–child interactions turn into conflicts when the child resists being fed or bathed or put to bed for a nap or bedtime. In one observational study of mother-child interaction, conflicts occurred on average 19 times an hour (Laible & Thompson, 2002).

Parents themselves may feel a surge of anger when the child is resisting something that has to be done; in very angry conflicts, both children and parents may resort to the use of force. At extreme levels, these angry conflicts lead to very difficult parent–child relationships.

Temper tantrums. Beginning in the second year of life, children may express their anger dramatically in the form of temper tantrums. Temper tantrums tie together general distress and frustration with anger (Giesbrecht, Miller, & Müller, 2010). The children cry, but may also hold their breath, bang their heads, or make noises to express their anger; for example, researchers have reported that 'There are children who grunt and growl and those whose shrieks reportedly sound to their parents like the cries of "a prehistoric bird"' (Potegal & Davidson, 2003, p. 140). When interviewed, parents reported that most tantrums lasted less than a minute, but that, when having a tantrum, some children became so wound up that they vomited or burst blood vessels in their eyes or cheeks. In those interviews, parents reported that most of the two- and three-year-olds had tantrums, but only about half of the four-year-olds did so.

Although many children have temper tantrums, not all have them at the same rate, and not all continue to have tantrums after the toddler years. For example, in a sample of over 1,000 children aged three- to five years visiting a paediatric clinic in a large city in the US, parents were asked whether their children had tantrums and, if so, whether these occurred rarely (less than once a week) or more often, up to more than once a day. About 80% of the children only rarely had tantrums, if at all. Fewer than 20% of these three- to five-year-olds were still regularly having tantrums, with only about 2% of children having them several times a day.

Similar findings emerged from a community sample of 861 one- to five-year-olds in Amsterdam (van den Akker, Hoffenaar, & Overbeek, 2022). When asked whether their child had ever had a tantrum, parents reported that most of the children did have tantrums, ranging from 78% in one-year-olds to 91% in three- and four-year-olds. Most of the children had had a tantrum in the last month. A minority of children had a tantrum every week or more than once in a given week.

The investigators used profile analysis to examine different patterns in these data. Just over a quarter of the children had a 'low intensity' profile; these children only infrequently had tantrums. Another group of children (32%) had a 'moderate intensity' profile, with elevated levels of distress as well as anger and physical aggression. The remaining children (42%) showed an 'aggressive/self-injurious' profile, engaging in self-harm as well as physical aggression against others. Thus, while virtually all of the children had tantrums, only some of them were harming themselves and others.

Angry Conflicts with Siblings and Peers

Conflicts with other children are common features of children's social lives. The conflicts children engage in with siblings and peers range from verbal arguments to physical fighting. Mild disagreements may escalate into angry attacks. Some children may hold long-lasting grudges that provoke a series of conflicts.

Conflict with siblings. Sibling conflict is ubiquitous in families with more than one child. These conflicts might take the form of mild disagreements, or they may escalate into physical fighting. Dramatic reports of sibling conflict have been written about since ancient times, such as the Biblical accounts of Cain killing his brother Abel and Joseph's brothers selling him into slavery (Vandell & Bailey, 1992).

In interviews about their childhood experiences, adults often note several positive effects of their quarrels with their siblings. For example, when adults were interviewed about their childhood relationships with their siblings, four out of five respondents reported positive outcomes of their disputes with their siblings (Bedford, Volling, & Avioli, 2000). However, one positive outcome that some parents reported was their understanding of the hurtfulness of their own conflicts with siblings and their attempts to support their own children by treating them as fairly as possible. These qualitative findings suggest that sibling conflict takes place in the context of complex parent–child relationships that may actually foster children's quarrels and difficulties in living in harmony with their siblings.

The birth of a sibling is a major life event for the eldest child in a family, and it is not surprising that firstborns initiate or respond more aggressively to conflicts with their siblings. For example, in a longitudinal study of siblings' interactions at home, firstborns were observed to be more aggressive than their younger siblings; both siblings' levels of aggressive behaviour were consistent over time (Martin & Ross, 1995). Sibling conflict is not rare, and these conflicts often feature physical aggression; surveys have shown that the percentage of families reporting sibling aggression ranges from 35% to 91% (Walters & Espelage, 2020). However, findings from some studies suggest that sibling conflict has some positive effects on children's development (Herrera & Dunn, 1997). These investigators suggested that conflict with siblings teaches children how to argue, as opposed to depending on the use of force, and understand social rules.

However, in a study of a low-income sample from a city in the US (Garcia, Shaw, Winslow, & Yaggi, 2000), destructive sibling conflict in addition to mothers' rejecting parenting style contributed to children's aggression, as reported by mothers and teachers. In other words, angry interactions between siblings increased the likelihood of aggression and conflict beyond the sibling relationship, in school as well as at home.

Conflicts with peers. Studies of infants' and toddlers' interactions with peers have generally shown that young children quite often resist or protest their peers' actions and sometimes use force against their peers. For example, in home observations of 1.5-year-old toddlers playing with a familiar peer, 67% of the focal children tugged toys held by the peers and 41% directed force against the peers' bodies (Hay et al., 2021). These conflicts were not one-sided: the more the focal child used force, the more the peer did as well.

Thus, in the toddler years, angry actions emerge when resources must be shared. Even in that period of development, however, individual differences are apparent and endure over time. As we shall see in the next chapter, angry toddlers may later develop clinically significant rage and aggressive behavioural problems that accelerate over the childhood years.

Genetic Influences and Gene–Environment Interactions

These individual differences in angry temperament are affected by a child's genetic heritage as well as the environment in which that child

Gene-environment Correlation

A concept that proposes that a person's choice of environment is associated with genetic factors. Individuals with particular genetic profiles may seek out and/or fare better in certain environments.

is growing up. In recent years, molecular geneticists have identified different genetic patterns that interact with a person's environment to influence that person's temperament. One of the most well-studied gene–environment interactions is that between the monoamine oxidase (MAOA) gene and the person's experience of maltreatment in childhood. In some longitudinal studies, this interaction between genetic patterns and the family environment has been found to predict the child's later antisocial behaviour and participation in criminal activities (e.g., Caspi et al., 2002; Ferguson et al., 2018).

The interaction between genetic profile and the quality of the home environment may depend on the quality of the parent–child relationship, not just other aspects of the home situation in which the child is growing up. For example, there is some evidence that the interaction between the MAOA gene and the child's early caregiving environment may affect the child's expressions of anger and readiness to engage in conflict with other people. For example, in a longitudinal study of families in the north of England, 14-month-old infants' tendencies to express anger were affected by an interaction between the child's MAOA genotype and the mothers' level of sensitivity to their infants (Pickles et al., 2013). This finding suggests that genetic influences on the development of children's anger are going to be modulated by features of children's home environments. This possibility is especially relevant for children who are on a trajectory toward uncontrollable rage and anger when in conflict with parents, siblings, teachers, and peers.

Further Reading

Lochman, J. E., Boxmeyer, C. L., Powell, N. P., Siddiqui, S., Stromeyer, S. L., & Sallee, M. (2024). Anger and aggression. In R. W. Christner & R. B. Mennuti (Eds.), *Cognitive behavioural interventions in educational settings: A handbook for practice* (3rd ed.). London: Routledge.

Liu, C., Moore, G. A., Beekman, C., Perez-Edgar, K. E., Leve, L. D., Shaw, D. S., Ganiban, J. S., Natsuaki, M. N., Reiss, D., & Neiderhiser, J. (2018). Developmental patterns of anger from infancy to middle childhood predict behavioural problems at age eight. *Developmental Psychology, 54*, 2090–2100.

References

Bedford, V. H., Volling, B. L., & Avioli, P. S. (2000). Positive consequences of sibling conflict in childhood and adulthood. *International Journal of Aging and Human Development, 51,* 1–84.

Bridges, K. M. B. (1932). Emotional development in early infancy. *Child Development, 3,* 324–331.

Caspi, A., McClay, J., Moffitt, T. E., Mill, J., Martin, J., Craig, I. W., Taylor, A., & Poulton, R. (2002). Role of genotype in the cycle of violence in maltreated children. *Science, 297,* 851–854.

Chaplin, T. M., & Aldao, A. (2013). Gender differences in emotion expression in children: A metanalytic review. *Psychological Bulletin, 39,* 735–765.

Ferguson, D. M., Boden, J. M., Horwood, L. J., Miller, A. L., & Kennedy, A. L. (2018). MAOA, abuse exposure, and antisocial behaviour: 30-year longitudinal study. *British Journal of Psychiatry, 198,* 466–472.

Garcia, M. M., Shaw, D. S., Winslow, E. B., & Yaggi, K. E. (2000). Destructive sibling conflict and the development of conduct problems in young boys. *Developmental Psychology, 36,* 44–53.

Giesbrecht, G. F., Miller, M. R., & Müller, U. (2010). The anger-distress model of temper tantrums: associations with emotional activity and emotional competence. *Infant and Child Development, 19,* 478–497.

Hay, D. F., Paine, A. L., Perra, O., Cook, K. V., Hashmi, S., Robinson, C., Kairis, V., & Slade, R. (2021). Prosocial and aggressive behaviour: A longitudinal study. *Monographs of the Society for Research in Child Development, 86,* Serial No. 341.

Hay, D. F., Perra, O., Hudson, K., Waters, C., Mundy, L., Goodyer, I., Harold, G., Thapar, A., & van Goozen, S. (2010). Identifying precursors to aggression: Psychometric properties of the Cardiff Infant Contentiousness Scale (CICS). *Aggressive Behaviour, 36,* 351–357.

Hay, D. F., & Ross, H. S. (1982). The social nature of early conflict. *Child Development, 53,* 105–113.

Herrera, C., & Dunn, J. (1997). Early experiences with family conflict: Implications for arguments with a close friend. *Developmental Psychology, 33,* 869–881.

Kerr, M. A., & Schneider, B. H. (2008). Anger expression in children and adolescents: A review of the empirical literature. *Clinical Psychology Review, 28,* 559–577.

Kochanska, G., Coy, K. C., Tjebkes, T. L., & Huserek, S. J. (2008). Individual differences in emotionality in infancy. *Child Development, 69,* 375–390.

Laible, D. J., & Thompson, R. A. (2002). Mother-child conflict in the toddler years: Lessons in emotion, morality, and relationships. *Child Development, 73,* 1187–1203.

Liu, C., Moore, G. A., Beekman, C., Perez-Edgar, K. E., Leve, L. D., Shaw, D. S., Ganiban, J. S., Natsuaki, M. N., Reiss, D., & Neiderhiser, J. (2018). Developmental patterns of anger from infancy to middle childhood Predict behavioural problems at age eight. *Developmental Psychology, 54,* 2090–2100.

Martin, J. L., & Ross, H. S. (1995). Sibling aggression: Sex differences and parents' reactions. *Early Education and Development, 6,* 335–358.

Pickles, A., Hill, J., Breen, G., Quinn, J., Abbott, K., Jones, H., & Sharp, H. (2013). Evidence for interplay between genes and parenting on infant temperament In the first year of life: Monoamine oxidase A polymorphism moderates effects of Maternal sensitivity on infant anger proneness. *Journal of Child Psychology and Psychiatry, 54,* 1308–1317.

Potegal, M., & Davidson, R. J. (2003). Temper tantrums in young children. I. Behavioral composition. *Journal of Developmental and Behavioral Pediatrics, 24,* 140–147.

Stenberg, C. R., Campos, J. J., & Emde, R. N. (1983). The facial expression of anger in seven-month-old infants. *Child Development, 54,* 178–184.

Vandell, D. L., & Bailey, M. D. (1992). Conflicts between siblings. In C. U. Shantz & W. W. Hartup (Eds.), *Conflict in child and adolescent development.* Cambridge: Cambridge University Press.

van den Akker, A. L., Hoffenaar, P., & Overbeek, G. (2022). Temper tantrums in toddlers and preschoolers: Longitudinal associations with adjustment problems. *Developmental Behavioral Pediatrics, 43,* 409–417.

Walters, G. D., & Espelage, D. L. (2020). Hostility, anger, and dominance as mediators of the sibling aggression-school fighting relationship: Mechanisms of violence generalization. *Psychology of Violence, 10,* 48–57.

Chapter 8

Difficult Temperament, Angry Aggressiveness, and Oppositional Defiant Disorder

As we have seen in the previous chapter, anger is a primary emotion that children as well as adults commonly experience from time to time. There are many reasons to get angry, and anger in itself is not a behavioural problem. Indeed, anger is often an appropriate response to the maltreatment of oneself or others and to acts of injustice. In childhood, many things may make children frustrated and angry, such as restrictions on their movements and activities, conflicts with parents and siblings, and conflicts with peers. Gradually, many children learn how to regulate their anger and settle conflicts in appropriate, nonviolent ways. However, some children continue to experience angry outbursts, and they may find it difficult to resolve conflicts without shouting or using force. Some of these angry children learn to engage in conflict without physical violence; others may persist in angry aggressiveness and are on the pathway to serious emotional and behavioural problems.

Difficult Temperament, Irritability, and Disruptive Mood Dysregulation Disorder (DMDD)

Some individual differences in expressing and regulating anger are already evident in the first year of life. They contribute to a pattern of emotions and behaviour that has been called 'difficult temperament' (Thomas, Chess, & Birch, 1968). Infants were considered to have 'difficult temperament' if their basic biological functioning seemed irregular, if they had problems adapting

Difficult Temperament

An informal label often given to a subgroup of children who have difficulties with regulating their emotions and engaging in harmonious interactions with their parents and other people, including other children. They may show anger and often engage in conflict with other people.

DOI: 10.4324/9781003483793-10

to changes in their environments, and if they often showed intense emotions and negative mood (Bates, 1980). These intense emotions included fussiness and protests, which are features of conflict between the infants and their parents and other caregivers (Olweus, 1984; Rubin et al., 1998).

One key feature of difficult temperament is the child's irritability, which has been defined as 'a low threshold for experiencing anger in response to frustration' (Brotman, Kircanski, & Leibenluft, 2017). Irritable people, both children and adults, are easily annoyed, often frustrated, and may have outbursts of temper (Ezpeleta et al., 2019). As we have seen in the previous chapter, temper tantrums are common in the first years of life, but they are not seen as expected behaviour in older children, adolescents, and adults. However, some people in all those age groups lose their tempers.

In the most recent set of definitions of mental health disorders (DSM-5), two aspects of irritability have been distinguished from each other: tonic and phasic irritability. 'Tonic irritability' is the term given to persistent, low-level angry moods, often referred to as grumpy or grouchy moods, a kind of baseline anger that may escalate into angry outbursts from time to time. The intense outbursts have been referred to as 'phasic irritability.' However, these two types of irritability are highly correlated (Copeland et al., 2015). Tonic irritability is more enduring than angry outbursts (Vidal-Ribas et al., 2016). Both types of irritability are included in the symptoms list of a new clinical diagnosis for children and adolescents that was introduced in DSM-5, 'disruptive mood dysregulation disorder' (DMDD). The symptoms of DMDD include severe recurrent temper outbursts and irritable or angry mood between outbursts.

This new DSM-5 diagnosis of DMDD is controversial (Dougherty et al., 2014). The symptoms overlap with other existing psychological disorders, including oppositional defiant disorder (ODD) and Attention Deficit and Hyperactivity Disorder (ADHD). However, this newer diagnosis draws attention to the links between behavioural and emotional problems in childhood and adolescence. This focus on emotional symptoms reminds us that children's and adolescents' anger may be related to other negative emotions such as sadness or depression, even though those other emotions are often expressed by means of aggression and other behavioural problems.

Individual Differences in Angry Aggressiveness

Longitudinal studies have revealed that individual differences in angry aggressiveness begin to emerge in the first year of life, with some children continuing to express their anger through the use of physical force in later childhood (Alink et al., 2006; Côté et al., 2006). Anger, of course, is a primary emotion that we all feel at times. However, some children

are more prone to anger than others, and some of those are particularly likely to express their anger by
using force against other people and
things. This early developing pattern of angry aggressiveness may set
a child on a trajectory toward more
severe behavioural problems at
home and in school (e.g., Brooker
et al., 2014; Hay et al., 2021;

Angry Aggressiveness

A tendency for some children
to express anger and engage
in verbal or physical aggression when interacting with
other people, including their
parents, siblings, and peers.

Lorber et al., 2014). This, in turn, may make it difficult for the child to
settle into school, make friends, and learn how to control his or her anger.

Such angry children may often not be living in a supportive environment that helps them regulate their emotions. Rather, angry aggressiveness is fostered by adverse home environments that are affected by
parents' own histories of anger and violence (e.g., Pawlby et al., 2011;
Pickles et al., 2013). Parents who have had such difficult experiences
may respond to the child's anger with their own bursts of anger, and
they may use physical punishments that actually escalate family conflicts.
Parents' and children's mental health is adversely affected by living in the
midst of such conflict, which may make it especially difficult for some
parents to suppress their own anger and help their children learn how
to manage their negative emotions. Angry responses to children's anger
may escalate into serious conflict, perhaps involving siblings as well as
parents. For example, in a longitudinal study that began in infancy and
followed up the children into primary school, the findings revealed that
the subset of children living in such conflict-ridden homes was at particular risk for later behavioural and emotional problems (Perra, Paine,
& Hay, 2021).

Oppositional Defiant Disorder

In contrast to the newer conceptualization of DMDD as a childhood
disorder that emphasizes emotional as well as behavioural problems,
Opposition-Defiant Disorder (ODD) is a well-established category of
emotional and behavioural problems that emerge in childhood, with the
symptoms listed in the fifth edition of the Diagnostic Statistical Manual
(DSM-5) published by the American Psychiatric Association. The diagnostic criteria for ODD are presented in Table 8.1. It is clear from the
symptoms described in the DSM-5 that ODD is a pattern of emotional
expression and social behaviour fuelled by anger.

Quite young children might receive diagnoses of Oppositional Defiant
Disorder; the diagnosis is often given to young children under the age of
eight. However, older children, adolescents, and even some adults also

receive diagnoses of ODD. The diagnostic criteria are somewhat different for young children compared to older children and teenagers. It may also be difficult to distinguish symptoms of ODD from angry outbursts in the early childhood years. Children who show common symptoms of ODD do not always receive formal diagnoses (Lin, He, Heath, Chin, & Hinshaw, 2022).

Research on ODD has drawn attention to the emotional underpinnings of children's oppositional behaviour, in particular their irritable temperaments. Gender differences are sometimes observed.

For example, in a web-based study of over 4,000 children (primarily nine-year-olds), whose behaviour was rated by parents (70%) or teachers (Cavanagh et al., 2014), boys were three times more likely than girls to meet the criteria for ODD. The children's symptoms of ODD were associated with problems they had in regulating their emotions. In that sample, emotional problems could be separated from the problematic behaviours that lead to diagnoses of conduct disorder, whereas ODD symptoms were associated with other types of emotional problems. These findings suggest that a subset of children who do not find it easy to rein in their tempers may have problems regulating other emotions as well. For this reason, ODD should be recognized as an emotional as well as a behavioural disorder.

Table 8.1 DSM Diagnostic Criteria for ODD

A. A pattern of angry/irritable mood, argumentative/defiant behaviour, or vindictiveness lasting at least six months, as evidenced by at least four symptoms from the following categories, and exhibited during interactions with at least one individual who is not a sibling:

Angry/Irritable Mood
1. Often loses temper
2. Is often touchy or easily annoyed
3. Is often angry and resentful

Argumentative/Defiant Behaviour
4. Often argues with authority figures or, for children and adolescents, with adults
5. Often actively defies or refuses to comply with requests from authority figures or with rules
6. Often deliberately annoys others
7. Often blames others for his or her mistakes or misbehaviour

Vindictiveness
8. Has been spiteful or vindictive at least twice within the past six months

---

Note: The persistence and frequency of these behaviours should be used to distinguish a behaviour that is within normal limits from a behaviour that is symptomatic. For children younger than five years, the behaviour should occur on most days for a period of at least six months unless otherwise noted (Criterion AB). For individuals five years or older, the behaviour should occur at least once per week for at least six months.

Prevalence of ODD Diagnoses

Although most young children do become angry and engage in conflict with parents and other people, formal diagnoses of ODD are not all that common in the general population (Hawes, Gardner, Dadds, Frick, Kimonis, Burke, & Fairchild, 2023). Between 3% and 4% of children meet the criteria for this diagnosis, as shown in meta-analyses of different studies in the last two decades (Canino et al., 2010; Vasileva et al., 2021). This relatively low prevalence of ODD is similar across different countries, for example in Europe, North America, China, and Iran (Hawes et al., 2023). However, in clinical samples of children who have been referred for help with their emotional or behavioural problems, over a third meet the criteria for ODD (Hawes et al., 2023).

In many samples of children, girls are somewhat less likely than boys to be diagnosed with ODD (the boy to girl ratio being 1.5 to 1). However, no gender differences were found in a Chinese sample (Lin et al., 2022). Adults also sometimes meet the criteria for ODD; in such adult samples, no gender differences are apparent (Johnston et al., 2018; Nock et al., 2007).

In general, findings from the studies of ODD suggest that a subset of children has particular difficulty controlling or growing out of anger and conflict with the people in their lives. Their strong opposition to other people's ideas and requests may endure into adulthood. Children who show various symptoms of ODD may have a particularly difficult time when they enter formal education, where they are expected to respond to teachers' directions and requests. Studies of young children's transitions to formal schooling might reveal a subgroup of children whose anger and irritability make it difficult to settle into their classrooms.

Emotional Features of ODD

The list of symptoms of ODD demonstrates that ODD is both an emotional and social disorder (Hawes, Gardner, Dadds, Frick, Kimonis, Burke, & Fairchild, 2023). The emotional symptoms are signs of irritability, including expressions of anger, loss of temper, and a general touchiness, i.e., as described informally, being easy to rile up. The remaining symptoms of ODD indicate that people with the diagnosis do not just feel angry, but act upon their anger by blaming, arguing, defying, annoying, and being spiteful toward other people. These symptoms are seen as both headstrong and hurtful. It may be difficult for children who are caught up in their own anger to consider the perspectives or needs of other people.

Although anger is a primary emotion that we all feel at times, the clinical diagnosis of ODD is not common in the general population. For example, two meta-analyses of different samples estimated that between 3% and 4% of the general population might meet the criteria for a diagnosis of ODD (Hawes et al., 2023). In contrast, between a third and half of the children and adolescents referred to mental health clinics for antisocial behaviour or in juvenile custody for illegal activities are likely to meet the diagnostic criteria for ODD.

Co-occurrence of ODD and ADHD

As we have seen, ODD is a clinically defined emotional disorder that emerges in early childhood. Some psychologists have investigated whether it might often co-occur with Attention Deficit and Hyperactivity Disorder (ADHD), which is also diagnosed in early to middle childhood. In psychiatric terminology, it is possible that ODD might be *comorbid* with ADHD.

One team of investigators hypothesized that there are two possible reasons why the two disorders might occur together (Harvey, Breaux, & Lugo-Candelas, 2016). One possibility is that ODD and ADHD might be influenced by the same risk factors, so they emerge in parallel in early childhood. A second possibility is that ADHD might be a developmental precursor to ODD; if so, children with ADHD symptoms might be more prone to engage in conflict with other people and disobey their parents and teachers.

Those investigators tested both possibilities in a longitudinal study, studying a sample of children who had already been shown to have behavioural problems (107 boys and 92 girls). Their analyses showed that earlier ADHD symptoms predicted subsequent ODD symptoms, partly because the children with ADHD symptoms were more likely to engage in family conflict, which provides situations that might foster the emergence of anger and related symptoms of ODD. In any case, joint symptoms of ADHD and ODD might make it quite difficult for children to regulate their attention and emotions in various contexts. In general, it is important to realize that children who show emotional problems may also have attentional and cognitive difficulties.

Further Reading

Hawes, D. J., Gardner, F., Dadds, M. R., Frick, P. J., Kimonis, E. R., Burke, J. D., & Fairchild, G. (2023). Oppositional Defiant Disorder. *Nature Reviews, 9*, Article No. 31.

References

Alink, L. R. A., Mesman, J., van Zeijl, J., Stolk, N. M., Juffer, F., Koot, H. M., Bakersmans-Kranenberg, & van Izendoorn, M. H. (2008). The early childhood aggression curve: Development of physical aggression in 10- to 50-month-old children. *Child Development, 77,* 954–966.

Bates, J.E. (1980). The concept of difficult temperament. *Merrill-Palmer Quarterly, 26,* 299–319.

Brotman, M., Kircanski, K., & Leibenluft, E. (2017). Irritability in children and adolescents. *Annual Review of Clinical Psychology, 13,* 317–341.

Brooker, R. J., Buss, K. A., Lemery-Chalfant, K., Aksan, N., Davidson, R., & Goldsmith, H. H. (2014). Profiles of observed infant anger predict preschool behavioral problems: Moderation by life stress. *Developmental Psychology, 50,* 2343–2352.

Canino, G., Polanczyk, G., Bauermeister, J. J., Rohde, L. A., & Frick, P. J. (2010). Does the prevalence of CD and ODD vary across cultures? *Social Psychiatry and Psychiatric Epidemiology, 45,* 695–704.

Cavanagh, M., Quinn, D., Duncan, D., Graham, T., & Balbuena, L. (2014). Oppositional defiant disorder is better conceptualized as a disorder of emotional regulation. *Journal of Attention Disorders, 21,* 381–389.

Copeland, W. E., Brofman, M. A., & Costello, E. J. (2015). Normative irritability in youth: Findings from the Great Smoky Mountains study. *Journal of the American Academy of Child & Adolescent Psychiatry, 54,* 635–642.

Côté, S., Vaillancourt, T., LeBlanc, J. C., Nagin, D. S., & Tremblay, R. E. (2006). The development of physical aggression from toddlerhood to preadolescence. *Journal of Abnormal Child Psychology, 34,* 71–85.

Dougherty, L. R., Smith, V. C., Bufferd, S. J., Kessel, E., Carlson, G. A., & Klein, D. N. (2014). Preschool irritability predicts child psychopathology, functional impairment, and service use at age nine. *Journal of Child Psychology and Psychiatry, 56,* 999–1007.

Ezpeleta, L., Penelo, E., de la Osa, N., Navarro, B., & Trepat, E. (2019). Irritability and parenting practices as mediational variables between temperament and affective, anxiety, and oppositional defiant problems. *Aggressive Behavior, 45,* 550–560.

Harvey, R. P., Breaux, E. A., & Lugo-Candelas, C. I. (2016). The role of parent psychopathology in emotion socialization. *Journal of Abnormal Child Psychology, 44,* 731–743.

Hawes, D. J., Gardner, F., Dadds, M. R., Frick, P. J., Kimonis, E. R., Burke, J. D., & Fairchild, G. (2023). Oppositional defiant disorder. *Nature Reviews, 9,* Article No. 31.AAA

Hay, D. F., Paine, A. L., Perra, O., Cook, K. V., Hashmi, S., Robinson, C., Kairis, V., & Slade, R. (2021). Prosocial and aggressive behaviour: A longitudinal study. *Monographs of the Society for Research in Child Development, 86,* Serial No. 341.

Johnston, O. G., Derella, O. J., & Burke, J. D. (2018). Identification of oppositional defiant Disorder in young adult college students. *Journal of Psychopathology and Behavioral Assessment, 40,* 563–572.

Lin, X., He, T., Heath, M., Chi, P., & Hinshaw, S. (2022). A systematic review of multiple family factors associated with oppositional defiant disorder. International *Journal of Environmental Research and Public Health, 19,* 10866.

Lorber, M. F., DelVecchio, T., & Slep, A. M. S. (2014). Infant externalizing behaviour as a self-organizing construct. *Developmental Psychology, 54,* 601.

Nock, M. K., Kazdin, A. E., Hiripi, E., & Kessler, R. C. (2007). Lifetime prevalence, correlates, and persistence of oppositional defiant disorder: results from the National Comorbidity Survey Replication. *Journal of Child Psychology and Psychiatry, 48,* 703–713.

Olweus, D. (1984). Stability in aggressive and withdrawn, inhibited behavior patterns. In R. M. Caplan, V. J. Konecni, & R. W. Novaco (Eds.), *Aggression in children and youth.* New York, NY: Springer.

Pawlby, S., Hay, D., Sharp., D., Waters, C. S., & Pariante, C. M. (2011). Antenatal depression and offspring psychopathology: The influence of childhood maltreatment. *British Journal of Psychiatry, 199,* 106–112.

Perra, O., Paine, A., & Hay, D. F. (2021). Continuity and change in anger and aggressiveness from infancy to childhood: The protective effects of positive parenting. *Development and Psychopathology, 33,* 937–956.

Pickles, A., Hill, J., Breen, G., Quinn, J., Abbott, K., Jones, H., & Sharp, H. (2013). Evidence for interplay between genes and parenting on infant temperament In the first year of life: Monoamine oxidase A polymorphism moderates effects of Maternal sensitivity on infant anger proneness. *Journal of Child Psychology and Psychiatry, 54,* 1308–1317.

Rubin, K. H., Hastings, P., Chen, X., Stewart, S., & McNichol, K. (1998). Intrapersonal and maternal correlates of aggression, conflict, and externalizing problems in toddlers. *Child Development, 69,* 1614–1629.

Thomas, A., Chess, S., & Birch, H. (1968). *Temperament and Behavior disorders in children.* New York, NY: New York University Press.

Vasileva, M., Graf, R. K., Reinelt, T., Petermann, U., & Petermann, F. (2021). Research review: A meta-analysis of the international prevalence and comorbidity of mental disorders in children between 1 and 7 years. *Journal of Child Psychology and Psychiatry, 62,* 372–381.

Vidal-Ribas, P., Brotman, M.A., Valdivieso, I., Leibenluft, E., & Stringaris, A. (2016). The status of irritability in psychiatry: A conceptual and quantitative review. *Journal of the American Academy of Child and Adolescent Psychiatry, 55,* 556–570.

Chapter 9

Empathy, Callousness, and Conduct Disorder

In contrast to ODD, which could be considered an emotional as well as a behavioural disorder defined by anger and opposition to the will of others, the list of symptoms of conduct disorder (CD) does not include anger or physical fighting (see Table 9.1). Rather, the list of CD symptoms consists of actions that violate the rights of other people, sometimes covertly and at other times in physically violent ways.

Many of the children who act in this way appear to lack empathy for other people. Children who are diagnosed with CD often show a lack of appropriate emotion and do not seem to understand how their behaviours may hurt others. Thus, to understand the pathways to these clinical problems, it is important first to focus on the development of two positive emotions: empathy and sympathy.

The Beginnings of Empathy

Infants' Emotional Reactions to Other People's Distress

In Chapter 2, when considering the early development of crying, we examined the phenomenon of 'contagious crying' where one infant's cry may trigger crying in another infant. This is often interpreted in terms of the second infant's finding the harsh sound of another infant's cry to be an unpleasant and perhaps frightening noise. It is certainly the case that older children and adults find infants' crying upsetting to listen to.

However, infants do not always respond to other infants' crying by becoming distressed themselves. For example, when pairs of six-month-old infants were observed together and one of the infants became distressed, the other infant was more likely to look toward the distressed infant's mother, not their own mothers, which would be more likely if they had become distressed themselves (Hay, Nash, & Pedersen, 1981). This pattern of looking toward the distressed infants' mothers rather than

DOI: 10.4324/9781003483793-11

their own mothers was also shown in a sample of 8-month-olds (Liddle et al., 2015).

Early Signs of Empathic Concern (and Lack of Concern) for Others

Empathic Concern

It is a prosocial emotion, characterized by feelings for a person who is distressed or having problems of some kind. Empathic concern requires being able to understand another person's perspective. Contagious crying in infants is not necessarily an example of early empathy; however, when infants and toddlers try to help a distressed person, perhaps by giving them their own toy, that is an early sign of empathic concern that can be deployed more effectively when children are older.

As young children grow older and acquire more motor skills, they often try to comfort people who have become distressed, often by doing something that their caregivers might do when the children themselves are in need of comfort. For example, toddlers might offer a teddy bear to an adult who is distressed (e.g., Hoffman, 1975). Such prosocial reactions were recorded in a study in which parents kept records of their children's responses to family members' distress (Zahn-Waxler et al., 1979). However, because naturally occurring distress is a low-frequency, unpredictable event, such naturalistic observations have been supplemented by studies in which experimenters simulate their own distress, e.g., pretending to hurt themselves by banging into furniture or catching their fingers in a drawer.

In one such study (Dunfield et al., 2011), in which the toddlers were given ten seconds to respond, no 18- or 24-month-old ever tried to comfort the experimenter, although some of the toddlers became distressed themselves. In another simulation study, in which two-year-olds' mothers simulated distress, the toddlers were more likely to react empathically to their own mothers than to the experimenters (Young et al., 1999). This is not always the case. For example, in a longitudinal study of young twins which included both mothers' and experimenters' simulations of distress, 14- to 36-month-olds showed empathic concern to experimenters as well as mothers (Knafo et al., 2008).

In another experiment, 12-, 18-, and 24-month-olds were shown realistic-looking baby dolls, along with an audio clip of a baby either crying or making contented cooing noises (Nichols, Svetlova, & Brownell, 2015). The 12-month-olds showed little reaction to the crying and the 18-month-olds were more likely to become distressed themselves than to try to express concern (although a few did). However, 67% of the 24-month-olds showed positive concern for the infant's distress, including behaviours described as 'positive social expression' (e.g., pointing to or otherwise calling attention to the infant, labelling it, or handing the baby doll a toy). Listening to the cooing sounds did not evoke either personal distress or concern for the infant. In that experiment, empathic concern for the infant was positively associated with empathic concern for the participants' own mothers when they simulated distress.

Evidence for empathic concern was also found when the crying doll procedure was replicated in a large community sample of British 24-month-olds (McHarg et al., 2019). In that representative sample, over half of the children showed mild or moderate concern for the very lifelike crying baby. Some of these two-year-olds attempted to soothe the baby doll.

More complex behavioural reactions to distress are seen when toddlers are studied with other young children, not experimenters or baby dolls. They may not respond empathically when confronted with their peers' distress, not least because they may be responsible for its occurrence. When peers become distressed, most young children are more likely simply to pay attention and perhaps attempt to react positively to their distressed peers (Demetriou & Hay, 2004; Lamb & Zakhirah, 1997). However, in those situations, some toddlers react to peers' distress with laughter or aggression. These reactions occur most often when young children have personally provoked their peers' distress, for example, by snatching away a toy (Demetriou & Hay, 2004; Zahn-Waxler et al., 1979).

Biological Factors That Influence Empathic Concern

Biological theorists have proposed that empathy for other people's emotions has evolved in the course of primate evolution. For example, Franz de Waal (2008) proposed that there were three levels of concern for others' emotions: 'emotional contagion' (such as contagious crying, as discussed above), 'sympathetic concern' (such as young children's attempts to soothe a crying baby doll, as discussed above), and 'empathic perspective-taking,' which requires understanding a person's emotions from that person's point of view. He argued that the first two levels could be discerned in the great apes, but the third was a developmental achievement for human children.

Some investigators have sought evidence for biological influences on young children's concern for other people's distress, testing for the influence of neurodevelopmental factors. For example, in a study that contrasted toddlers who were at high and low genetic risk for autism (i.e., those who did or did not have a sibling who had been diagnosed with autism), those toddlers at lower risk showed more empathic concern in response to a crying baby than did the children who had siblings with ASD diagnoses. The children at lower risk were also more likely to respond to an adult's simulation of pain. There were also group differences in language and communication skills, but those variables did not completely explain the group difference in empathic concern (Campbell et al., 2015).

Another biological mechanism thought to promote empathy is the hormone oxytocin (e.g., Uzefovsky et al., 2015). Molecular genetic analyses revealed a link between the oxytocin receptor gene and young children's tendencies to help and comfort other people. However, in another study, the oxytocin receptor gene was not related to children's likelihood of engaging prosocially with others through sharing (Wu & Su, 2015). Taken together, these findings suggest that there may be some biological influences on the development of feelings of empathy, perhaps as opposed to other facets of prosocial behaviour, but the causal picture is quite complex.

Perspective-Taking, Theory of Mind, and Cognitive Empathy

With respect to de Waal's contention that perspective-taking is a developmental achievement for human children, it is clear that children only gradually develop an understanding of other people's needs and feelings. Over the preschool years and into middle childhood, children gradually become better able to recognize and understand other people's emotions. By the time they are five years old, many children can recognize people's happiness from their facial expressions (e.g., Gau & Maurer, 2010). However, they have more difficulties in decoding people's expressions of negative emotions. It seems to be particularly difficult for children to recognize another person's anger (Herba, Landau, Russell, Ecker, & Phillips, 2006).

For example, in a study of children and teenagers ranging in age from 5 to 15, the participants were asked to match drawings of faces expressing different emotions (Gau & Maurer, 2010). The faces were presented without any hair and without labelling their gender. In general, the participants were easily able to match faces that expressed happiness or fear but were less likely to match faces expressing anger. Whereas the majority of children and teenagers could match happy or fearful faces, only 57% of young children could do so. This implies that when interacting with people who were feeling different emotions, children would not always be able to see that another person was angry, which might in itself lead to conflict. The youngest children also found it difficult to process expressions of disgust and sadness. These findings suggest that children's empathic reactions to other people's emotions might first be seen in relation to fearfulness, perhaps because the situation is frightening them as well, but only later in response to anger, disgust, or sadness.

It is also the case that children's reactions to other people's distress are complicated, particularly if the child in question was somehow responsible for provoking the distress. In this kind of situation, children may experience other emotions that are centred on themselves, not the person whom they have distressed. They may not understand the link between their actions and the other person's distress. If they do understand that they had a hand in making another person so upset, they may feel shame or guilt.

Shame and Guilt

As we have seen in the previous chapters, primary emotions such as fear or anger are already being expressed in infancy and continue to be expressed throughout our lifetimes. The primary emotions are usually triggered by specific events and environmental cues of danger or restrictions or attacks on your person or possessions (e.g., being left alone in an unfamiliar environment; having a favourite possession grabbed out of your hand).

In contrast, as children grow older, their own actions might provoke more complicated feelings. These feelings of shame and guilt are referred to as 'self-conscious emotions.' In early childhood, children gradually develop a sense of self. During early childhood, they begin to recognize their own agency and understand that their physical actions and verbal comments may hurt other people, either physically or psychologically.

Some children may not see anything wrong with what they've done and continue to behave in ways that upset other people. Other children become upset by their own

Shame and Guilt

These are both moral emotions that are felt after having done something wrong, but they differ in terms of the person's own feelings about the wrongness of their actions. People may feel shame if they know that what they've done is wrong and if others also know about their transgression. If what they did was only a mild mistake, only feel embarrassment. However, mistakes have effects on other people's feelings: a person who feels shame is upset about being seen negatively by other people. Guilt is a stronger feeling about having transgressed and, in doing so, harming other people. The person who feels guilt is engaging in a form of perspective-taking, focusing on what happened to other people, how they might feel about it, and how, if possible, they might make amends. In other words, guilty feelings are about the harm done to other people.

actions, especially when their wrongdoing is pointed out to them by parents and other adults, and when they receive some punishment for what they did.

Some of the actions that upset other people are accidental; others are deliberate. Even accidental actions such as tripping over a kerb and then making a mess by dropping a bag of groceries onto the street might provoke feelings of shame. This is particularly likely to be the case if other people have witnessed the mess and are calling attention to the person who caused the problem.

In other cases, such as deliberately throwing a tomato at someone else in the context of an escalating argument, the tomato thrower might (or might not) feel guilty for having lost control of her behaviour. She might (or might not) feel the need to make reparations for her actions. People who feel guilt may then attempt to solve the problems they have created. This suggests that people who experience guilt may feel some empathy for the other people who have been affected by their actions.

Shame and guilt are part of a category of self-conscious emotions that also include embarrassment, pride, and envy (Mills, 2005). It could be said, however, that a child's feelings of shame and guilt could also be described as 'other-conscious emotions,' based on the awareness that other people are watching and perhaps judging. Children's complex feelings of shame and guilt may develop in parallel with their growing understanding that other people also have thoughts and feelings that may be judgemental. They are key elements in the development of moral understanding:

Shame

In recent years, psychologists have discovered that these moral emotions develop earlier than previously believed. Some signs of shame emerge before the second birthday and may indeed have their origins in the first year (Draghi-Lorenz, Reddy, & Costall, 2001).

Shame is often described as a self-conscious emotion, combining feelings about oneself with awareness of the social context of other people's actions and judgements. It has been defined as:

> a painful emotion characterized by the concern about the others' judgment on the self, the awareness of appearing in front of an audience in an undesired or not approved way ('unwanted identity') and is typically accompanied by a sense of shrinking or of 'being small,' of worthlessness and powerlessness.
>
> (Menesini & Camodeca, 2008)

Various theorists have agreed that shame and the other self-conscious emotions require cognitive abilities that emerge after infancy. However, toddlers' feelings when adults or older children laugh at them surely are manifestations of shame.

Guilt

Feelings of guilt emerge between two and three years of age when individual differences have already begun to be present. For example, in a study of two- to five-year-old children who visited a developmental lab in the Netherlands (Nikolic, Brummelman, de Castro, Jorgensen, & Colonnesi, 2023), the children were led to believe that they had accidentally broken the experimenter's favourite toy. They were then told that the experimenter needed help.

The investigators had hypothesized that children's verbal and non-verbal signs of shame or guilt would be related to their understanding of social interactions. In particular, they predicted that the parents' warmth and references to mental states when talking to their children might promote both positive social behaviour and, under these circumstances, the children's expressions of guilt. They also hypothesized that the children who expressed feelings of guilt might help the experimenter, which did, in fact, happen. In contrast, the children who had shown signs of shame as opposed to guilt were less likely to help the experimenter.

In another study of children's feelings of shame and guilt, carried out in an older sample of 102 9- to 11-year-old children recruited in the area around Florence, Italy, the investigators asked questions about shame and guilt in relation to the children's experiences of bullying and victimization, and also prosocial behaviour (Menesini & Camodeca, 2008). The children were asked to respond to scenarios that might evoke either shame or guilt. They also participated in a peer nomination task that yielded categories of bullies, victims, prosocial actors, or uninvolved members of their classrooms. Boys were more often bullies and girls more often prosocial actors, but there were no gender differences in the victim or uninvolved groups.

Younger children were more likely than the older children to say they would experience shame in embarrassing situations such as falling asleep in class. Children in the prosocial group were most likely to say they would experience shame as well as guilt in the different situations. As might be expected, the bullies were least likely to express either shame or guilt. The children who were characterized as not involved in the classroom dynamics were also less likely to report that they would feel shame or guilt.

A cross-sectional study like this does not explain why children become bullies or especially prosocial actors, or withdraw from participation in classroom activities, but it does suggest that feelings of shame and guilt, or their absence, are important for school-aged children's social relations.

Children with Callous-Unemotional Traits

Callous-Unemotional Traits

These include the absence of empathic concern, but also a lack of remorse or guilt, shallow affect, and callousness, with little regard for other people's well-being. People with CU traits are unlikely to help other people in distress and do not feel guilty if they themselves perpetrate the distress. These traits are often associated with a clinical diagnosis of psychopathy.

In recent years, clinicians have identified a subset of children who seem to be especially callous in relation to other people's sadness and distress. Their behaviour stands in contrast to the evidence for the development of concern for others. As we have seen, infants and young children often become distressed when another person is upset and sometimes try to comfort people who are sad, even though they are not yet able to discern what those people actually need. As they grow older, most children gain knowledge about how to help and comfort other people. However, some children react to other people's injuries or emotional problems with callousness, sometimes acting to make the situation worse. Such children are said to have 'callous-unemotional traits' (Viding & Kimonis, 2018).

Children's callous-unemotional (CU) traits are typically measured via questionnaires that have been completed by parents, teachers, or other people who know the children well (e.g., Frick et al., 2014). Factor analyses of the questionnaire items yield three dimensions: being uncaring about others, being unemotional, and being callous in response to people's problems. Children with high levels of CU traits tend to be more aggressive than other children in general. When compared with other aggressive children, children with CU traits have more severe behavioural problems and, unsurprisingly, show less prosocial behaviour at home and in school (Hay et al., 2021). Neurocognitive analyses of brain patterns have shown that, compared to typically developing children, the children with CU traits show less activity in the amygdala when presented with photos of people with fearful facial expressions (Viding & Kimonis, 2018). In comparison with other children who engage in antisocial behaviour, children with CU traits experience fewer feelings of guilt.

Diagnoses of Conduct Disorder in Childhood and Adolescence

Onset of CD in Childhood

The evidence on the development of anger, combined with the evidence on callous-unemotional traits, indicates that there are different subsets of children who meet the criteria for conduct disorder. For those children who meet the criteria for both ODD and CD, their high levels of anger may fuel angry outbursts and physical aggression. The list of symptoms in the DSM-5 definition of CD includes physical violence, which certainly could be accompanied by anger, but also incorporates other ways of harming others, including the use of weapons and sexual abuse (see Table 9.1).

Other CD symptoms include nonviolent but destructive behaviours such as stealing other people's property, setting fires, or breaking into houses and shops; forging documents; breaking rules set by parents

Table 9.1 Symptoms of Conduct Disorder

A. A repetitive and persistent pattern of behaviour in which the basic rights of others or major age-appropriate societal norms or rules are violated, as manifested by the presence of three (or more) of the following 15 criteria in the past 12 months from any of the categories below, with at least one criterion present in the past six months:

Aggression to people and animals

1. Often bullies, threatens, or intimidates others
2. Often initiates physical fights
3. Has used a weapon that can cause serious physical harm to others (e.g., a bat, brick, broken bottle, knife, and gun)
4. Has been physically cruel to people
5. Has been physically cruel to animals
6. Has stolen while confronting a victim (e.g., mugging, purse snatching, extortion, and armed robbery)
7. Has forced someone into sexual activity

Destruction of property

8. Deliberately engages in fire-setting with the intent to cause serious damage
9. Deliberately destroys others' property (other than by fire-setting)

Deceitfulness or theft

10. Lies or "cons" others to obtain goods or favors or to avoid obligations
11. Breaks into someone's house, building, or car
12. Steals items of non-trivial value without confronting a victim (e.g., shoplifting)

Serious violations of rules

13. Stays out at night despite parental prohibitions, beginning before age 13
14. Runs away from home overnight at least twice, or runs away once without returning for a long period
15. Is frequently truant from school

or society at large. These activities indicate levels of callousness, self-centredness, and a lack of empathy toward other people. Both violent and nonviolent symptoms of conduct disorder are signs that the people committing these inconsiderate actions are acting callously, not caring about other people's needs. Thus, a lack of empathy for others underlies the development of conduct disorder, even when the person is not in a rage or performing acts of violence against the victims. We should note, however, that many children meet the criteria for a combined diagnosis of ODD and CD, which suggests they may have angry outbursts but also engage in other forms of antisocial behaviour (Table 9.1).

Emotional Processing and Conduct Disorder

The factors that trigger the onset of CD have been thought to be different in early childhood versus adolescence. are thought to be different from the dare different in adolescence. For example, children whose behavioural problems are evident in the early childhood years were thought to have *life-course persistent* CD as opposed to *adolescent-onset* CD (Moffitt, 1993). Young people whose conduct symptoms began early and those whose symptoms emerged in adolescence may both find it difficult to express their feelings and understand other people's emotions. However, some of the problems in expressing and interpreting other people's emotions are experienced by adolescents whose conduct problems have escalated in the teenage years, as well as those individuals whose behaviour has been problematic since early childhood.

For example, in a comparison of three groups of teenage boys who had been diagnosed with CD either in childhood or more recently in adolescence, or did not meet the criteria for CD, or who had not experienced these disorders or other mental health problems (Fairchild, van Goozen, Calder, Stollery, & Goodyer, 2009), all the boys were tested on their abilities to recognize photographs of faces and the specific emotional expressions shown on those faces. The three groups of boys did not differ in being able to recognize the identity of the faces they were presented with. Nor did they differ in the ability to recognize sad or surprised faces.

The boys whose conduct problems had emerged in the teenage years had difficulty in recognizing fear and some nonsignificant problems in recognizing anger, compared to the boys who did not have conduct problems. However, they had no problems recognizing happiness and disgust. In contrast, those boys whose conduct problems began early in childhood had difficulties in recognizing happiness, disgust, fear, and anger. In other words, those boys whose behavioural problems had emerged early in childhood had fewer skills in decoding facial expressions of emotions, which might make it more difficult to feel empathic toward other people's feelings.

Other Emotional Problems and Conduct Disorder

Subsequent research in other samples that have included girls and boys has found that the emotional problems affecting individuals with CD go beyond these problems in recognizing and understanding people's facial expressions. For example, in the large, multi-site FEM-Nat CD sample of 542 9- to 18-year-olds who had been diagnosed with CD and 710 girls and boys in the same age range, the investigators also measured the participants' abilities for emotional regulation and emotional learning (Kohls et al., 2000). The investigators hypothesized that different types of adverse experiences would affect children's emotional development in different ways, which leads to different subgroups of children. They all might meet the diagnostic criteria for CD yet may have other sets of social and emotional problems that need to be dealt with in different ways.

For example, these investigators noted that problems in recognizing other people's emotions are often seen in the subgroup of individuals who show callous-unemotional traits and are less likely to show any positive, prosocial emotions. They suggested that a history of abuse and/or neglect might limit children's abilities to recognize and interpret other people's emotions. In particular, children who had been abused or neglected might find it quite difficult to recognize and understand positive emotions in other people. They might see positive overtures as threats. Alternatively, children who have been physically abused might be very good at recognizing anger as a signal of oncoming attacks.

However, in a systematic review of studies of maltreated children (Assed et al., 2019), different patterns were seen across the studies. In general, children with better cognitive skills were more accurate in recognizing emotional expressions, even if they had experienced maltreatment. However, the nature of the maltreatment mattered. Across the studies, those children who had suffered from physical abuse were generally able to recognize anger, sometimes with very few cues (e.g., Ardizzi et al., 2015). In contrast, children who had experienced neglect were less accurate in recognizing different emotions, including anger (Pollak et al., 2000). Taken together, these findings suggest that individuals' childhood experiences can create difficulties and biases in emotion processing, which will affect their later social skills and social understanding.

Young People Who Commit Brutal Assaults and Homicide

With luck, children with conduct problems may find supportive programmes that help reduce their anger and encourage them to control their aggressive impulses. However, some of the children with conduct problems are unable to find such support or do not seem to benefit from their participation in prevention or intervention programmes designed to reduce their anger and violent impulses. Such children often engage in physical fighting and then may go on to commit physical assaults on victims. Crime records reveal that a proportion of young people, most with a history of conduct problems, engage in physical fights and attack victims whom they may or may not know personally. Such attacks may result in severe injuries for the victims or, in some cases, the victim's death.

What factors earlier in development might predict which young people commit homicide? Investigators attempted to answer this question by analysing data collected longitudinally in the Pittsburgh Youth Study in the US, a longitudinal study of boys' development that began in 1987 when the boys were in primary school (Farrington, Loeber, & Berg, 2012). At the beginning of the study, the investigators drew samples from three cohorts with averages of 7, 10 and 13 years. The participants were then followed up over time, with information on those who had committed homicide by 2009; 37 participants (2% of the sample) had done so.

Those young men who had killed others were likely to have grown up in disadvantaged neighbourhoods, often with a young single parent. They had an early history of disruptive behaviour disorders and had a positive attitude toward engaging in delinquent behaviour. They had been engaging in crime since their mid-teenage years, at rates that were significantly higher than the criminal activities of the rest of the sample. These findings suggest that homicidal youth were growing up in difficult environments where engagement in lesser crimes began early in development; in contrast to other members of the sample, most of the homicidal men had a long history of violence before they were 14 years old.

In the UK, rates of violent crime had declined from levels in the 1990s but have risen again since 2014, with the majority of such crimes being perpetrated by young people, particularly those who have become members of gangs (Haylock, Boshari, Alexander, Kumar, Manikam, & Pinder, 2020).

Violent Crime

In the UK, violent crime is defined as offences that involve physical force or the threat of force against people, leading to harm, injury and the fear of harm. Such crimes include homicide, assault, sexual offences and robbery.

Further Reading

Decety, J., & Holvoet, C. (2021). The emergence of empathy: A developmental neuroscience perspective. *Developmental Review, 62,* 100999.

Frick, P. J., & Kemp, E. C. (2021). Conduct disorders and empathy development. *Annual Review of Clinical Psychology, 17,* 391–416.

References

Ardizzi, A., Martini, F., Ulmilta, M. A., Evangelista, V., Ravera, R., & Galese, V. (2015). Impact of childhood maltreatment on the recognition of facial expressions of emotion. *PLoS One, 10,* e0141732.

Assed, M. M., Khalif, T. C., Belizario, G. O., Fatorelli, R., Castanho de Ameida Rocca, C., & de Padua Serafim, A. (2020). Facial emotion recognition in maltreated children: *Journal of Child and Family Studies, 29,* 1493–1509.

Campbell, S., Leezenbaum, M. B., Schmidt, E. N., Day, T. N., & Brownell, C. (2015). Concern for another's distress in toddlers at low and high genetic risk for Autism Spectrum Disorder. *Journal of Autism and Developmental Disorders, 45,* 3594–3605.

Demetriou, H., & Hay, D. F. (2004). Toddlers' reactions to the distress of familiar peers: The importance of context. *Infancy, 6,* 299–318.

de Waal, F. B. M. (2008). Putting the altruism back into altruism: The evolution of empathy. *Annual Review of Psychology, 59,* 279–300.

Draghi-Lorenz, R., Reddy, V., & Costall, A. (2001). Rethinking the development of 'nonbasic' emotions: A critical review of existing theories. *Developmental Review, 21,* 263–304.

Dunfield, K. A., Kuhlmeier, V. A., O'Connell, L., & Kelley, E. (2011). Examining the diversity of prosocial behaviour: Helping, sharing, and comforting in infancy. *Infancy, 16,* 227–247.

Fairchild, G., van Goozen, S. H., Calder, A. J., Stollery, S. J., & Goodyer, I. M. (2009). Deficits in facial expression recognition in male adolescents with early-onset or adolescent-onset conduct disorder. *Journal of Child Psychology and Psychiatry, 50,* 627–636.

Farrington, D. P., Loeber, R., & Berg, M. T. (2012). Young men who kill: A prospective longitudinal examination from childhood. *Homicide Studies, 16,* 99–128.

Frick, P. J., Ray, J. V., Thornton, L. C., & Kahn, R. E. (2014). Can callous-unemotional traits enhance the understanding, diagnosis, and treatment of serious conduct problems in children and adolescents? A comprehensive review. *Psychological Bulletin, 140,* 1–57.

Gau, X., & Maurer, D. (2010). A happy story: Developmental changes in children's sensitivity to facial expressions of varying intensities. *Journal of Experimental Child Psychology, 107,* 67–86.

Hay, D. F., Nash, A., & Pedersen, J. (1981). Responses of six-month-olds to the distress of their peers. *Child Development, 52,* 1071–1076.

Hay, D. F., Paine, A. L., Perra, O., Cook, K. V., Hashmi, S., Robinson, C., Kairis, V., & Slade, R. (2021). Prosocial and aggressive behavior: A longitudinal study. *Monographs of the Society for Research in Child Development, 86,* 7–103.

Haylock, S., Boshari, T., Alexander, E. C., Kumar, A., Manikam, L., & Pinder, R. (2020). Risk factors associated with knife crime in United Kingdom among young people aged 10-24 years: a systematic review. *BMC Public Health, 20,* 1–19.

Herba, C. M., Landau, S., Russell, T., Ecker, C., & Philips, M. L. (2006). The development of emotion processing in children: Effects of age, emotion, and intensity. *Journal of Child Psychology and Psychiatry, 47,* 1098–1106.

Hoffman, M. L. (1975). Developmental synthesis of affect and cognition and its implications for altruistic motivation. *Developmental Psychology*, *11*, 607–622.

Knafo, A., Zahn-Waxler, C., van Hulle, C., Robinson, J. L., & Rhee, S. H. (2008). The developmental origins of a disposition toward empathy: Genetic and environmental contributions. *Emotion*, *8*, 737–752.

Kohls, G., Fairchild, G., Bernhard, A., Martinelli, A., Smaragdi, A., Gonzalez-Madruga, K., Wells, A., Rogers, J. C., Pauli, R., Oldenhof, H., Jansen, L., Rhijn, A. van, Kersten, L., Alfano, J., Baumann, S., Herpertz-Dahlmann, B., Vetro, A., Lazaratou, H., Hervas, A., ... Konrad, K. (2020). Neuropsychological subgroups of emotion processing in youths with conduct disorder. *Frontiers in Psychiatry*, *11*.

Lamb, S., & Zakhireh, B. (1997). Toddlers' attention to the distress of peers in a daycare setting. *Early Education and Development*, *8*, 105–118.

Liddle, M.-J. E., Bradley, B. S., & Mcgrath, A. (2015). Baby empathy: Infant distress and peer prosocial responses. *Infant Mental Health*, *36*, 446–458.

McHarg, G., Fink, E., & Hughes, C. (2019). Crying babies, empathic toddlers, responsive mothers and fathers: Exploring parent-toddler interactions in an empathy paradigm. *Journal of Experimental Child Psychology*, *179*, 23–37.

Menesini, E., & Camodeca, M. (2008). Shame and guilt as behaviour regulators: Relationships with bullying, victimization and prosocial behaviour. *British Journal of Developmental Psychology*, *26*, 183–196.

Mills, R. S. L. (2005). Taking stock on the developmental literature on shame. *Developmental Review*, *25*, 26–63.

Moffitt, T. E. (1993). The neuropsychology of conduct disorder. *Development and Psychopathology*, *5*, 135–151.

Nichols, S., Svetlova, M., & Brownell, C. A. (2015). Toddlers' responses to infants' negative emotions. *Infancy*, *20*, 70–97.

Nikolic, M., Brummelman, E., Orobio de Castro, B., Jorgensen, T. D., & Colonnesi, C. (2023). Parental socialization of guilt and shame in early childhood. *Scientific Reports*, *13*, Article number 11767.

Pollak, S. D., Cicchetti, D., Hornung, K., & Reed, A. (2000). Recognizing emotion in faces: Developmental effects of child abuse and neglect. *Developmental Psychology*, *36*, 679–688.

Uzefovsky, F., Shalov, I., Israel, S., Edelman, S., Raz Y., Mankuta, D., Knafo Noem, A., & Ebstein, R. P. (2015). Oxytocin receptor and vasopressin receptor 1a genes are respectively associated with emotional and cognitive empathy. *Hormones and Behavior*, *67*, 60–65.

Viding, E., & Kimonis, E. R. (2018). Callous-unemotional traits. In C. J. Patrick (Ed.), *Handbook of psychopathy* (2nd ed., pp. 144–164). London: Guilford.

Wu, S., & Su, N. (2015). Oxytocin receptor gene relates to theory of mind and prosocial behavior in children. *Journal of Cognition and Development*, *16*, 302–315.

Young, S. K., Fox, N. A., & Zahn-Waxler, C. (1999). The relations between temperament and empathy in two-year-olds. *Developmental Psychology*, *35*, 1189–1197.

Zahn-Waxler, C., Radke-Yarrow, M., & King, R. A. (1979). Child-rearing and children's prosocial initiations to victims of distress. *Child Development*, *50*, 319–330.

Chapter 10

Sadness

Sadness is considered to be a primary emotion, a feeling that we experience in response to our past or present losses, which may create pessimistic expectations for our futures. Our feelings of sadness encompass our grief in response to bereavements and feeling sad about the loss of important relationships or future opportunities. Nostalgia for people we used to know and places where we used to live will provoke feelings of sadness, even if within our present circumstances, we are leading quite happy lives.

Sadness is felt in the body. Our feelings of sadness are communicated to others by way of our facial expressions and postures. For example, as a team of neuroscientists described the visible signs of sadness:

> In humans, sadness is characterised by specific behaviours (social withdrawal, lower reward seeking, slow gait), a typical facial expression (drooping eyelids, downcast eyes, lowered lip corners, slanting inner eyebrows), physiological changes (heart rate, skin conductance) as well as cognitive/subjective processes.
>
> (Arias et al., 2020, p. 199)

Darwin referred to the muscles producing the facial expression of sadness as the 'grief muscles.' Sadness is also expressed by the voice…crying, ululating in grief, and singing laments in the face of loss.

Children feel sad in response to unpleasant things that happen to them, particularly to adverse experiences that are beyond their control. Investigators of children's sadness have noted that:

> Sadness is usually elicited by adverse events, such as being rejected, losing something, or simply not getting what you want; evaluating an event as negative and themselves as powerless to reverse the outcome or change the situation's triggered by particular events.
>
> (Duarte, Brito, & Reis, 2016)

DOI: 10.4324/9781003483793-12

It is the lack of power that makes children feel sad, when they can either face the unpleasant situation with angry protests or run away from the situation out of fear. When neither fight nor flight is possible, children may just feel sad.

Sad Facial Expressions in Infancy

It can be challenging to identify sadness in infants. Some facial expressions that signify sadness can be observed in the first two years of life, but infants' sad expressions are less common than their expressions of fear, frustration, and happiness. Emotion researchers have noted that it is not always possible to distinguish infants' expressions of sadness from their expressions of other emotions (Izard et al., 1995; Oster et al., 1992). As the infants grow older, crying in distress becomes differentiated, communicating fear, or anger, or sadness, or perhaps more than one of those emotions. Even temper tantrums may contain an element of sadness, whining and fussing rather than shouting at other people (Green, Whitney, & Potegal, 2011).

Sadness Induced by Frustration

Infants as well as older children often express sadness in response to frustrating circumstances. For example, in one laboratory experiment (Lewis et al., 1992), infants were taught to pull a string to see a photograph of a smiling baby, accompanied by the theme tune to the children's television programme *Sesame Street*. After doing this for three minutes, the infants found that pulling on the string no longer worked. About half of the infants reacted to their loss of agency with a mixture of sad and angry facial expressions. Other infants expressed only anger or only sadness.

Older children similarly react with anger and/or sadness when frustrated. Some investigators have proposed that children who have angry reactions to frustration may be more likely to persist in trying to solve the problem, whereas children who react with sadness may simply abandon the task and move on to something else (e.g., Lewis et al., 2015). This response may be underpinned by feelings of helplessness, which might lower the children's self-esteem. As they grow up, children will periodically experience upsetting situations that they are helpless to avoid or fix, which may indeed contribute to their feelings of competence and self-worth.

Sadness in Response to Loss

Sadness is an emotion that is often triggered by loss of one sort or another. This can be a temporary or permanent loss, and in the case of permanent losses such as bereavement, sadness may be expressed as enduring grief. However, even the temporary loss of the presence of another person can make us sad.

Brief Separations from Parents and Other Caregivers

Infants' expressions of sadness have been observed during an experimental paradigm designed to assess different patterns of infants' attachment relationships with their primary caregivers (usually their mothers), which is called the Strange Situation. The Strange Situation is composed of brief episodes in which infants are observed on their own with their mothers, then in the company of the mother and an unfamiliar person, then when their mothers leave the room, and then when mothers and infants are reunited (Ainsworth & Bell, 1970).

Sometimes separation can evoke mixed emotions. In one such study of brief separations, infants' facial expressions of both anger and sadness were recorded when their mothers left the room (Shiller, Izard, & Hembree, 1986). In that sample, sadness, as opposed to anger, was more frequent in the subgroup of infants who met criteria for insecure attachment.

Brief Separations

The emotional effects of children's separation from their family members and familiar companions vary in intensity. Brief, regular separations between children and their family members are common. These routine separations often begin in infancy, when infants may be cared for by others during the working day and become increasingly common as the child grows older. However, when families move house, children may be permanently separated from their friends.

Longer-Term Separations from Parents

In childhood, many children will experience separation from their parents, both brief separations when their parents go out for the evening or daily separations when parents go to work. Some children also experience longer-term separations from the family home. Some of these separations have come about from

Longer Separations

Longer separations from family members, such as going to summer camps or boarding schools, may often induce sadness and loneliness. There are individual differences in feelings about such temporary but longer separations.

parents' decisions to provide children with potentially positive recreational and educational experiences, such as attending a summer camp or going to a boarding school. Other separations have arisen due to life events within the family that have led to separation from one or both parents.

Summer camps. During the school holidays, particularly in North America, it is quite common for children to spend some time at camps where they may engage in various sports, go on nature hikes, play music or put on plays, depending on the offerings at a given camp. Some children attend day camps, but others go to what is known as 'sleepaway camps,' thus leaving the family home for a week or more. Many children enjoy their time at camp, but others find the separation from their families emotionally challenging, experiencing a specific kind of sadness that adults refer to as 'homesickness.'

For example, in a study of 275 children attending a week-long stay at a summer camp in upstate New York, USA (Kingery, Penesten, Rice, & Wormuth, 2012), researchers asked children to answer questionnaires (which were read out to the younger children) about their camp experiences. The children reported on their feelings of anxiety and homesickness. The investigators had also asked parents to report whether they were anxious about their child's reactions to being at camp and whether the child had been involved in the decision to go to camp. The children's reports of homesickness were positively associated with their feelings of anxiety and also with their parents' own feelings of anxiety. Thus, in this sample, the children's feelings of sadness at the separation from their parents were bound up with levels of anxiety in both child and parent. This suggests that this subgroup of children was responding to the separation with fearfulness as well as sadness.

Boarding Schools

Longer periods of separation from parents and other family members occur when children and adolescents are sent to boarding schools where they live at school during term time. Studies using retrospective reports from individuals who attended boarding schools have identified 'boarding school syndrome' (Partridge, 2021).

A key question about children's experiences being educated away from their family homes is whether life in boarding school affects their understanding and regulation of their emotions. For example, in a sample of seven- to ten-year-old children in a private boarding school in China, the child participants were asked to respond to vignettes that contained examples of characters' happiness, sadness, anger, and fear (Rao & Gibson, 2018). In this sample, children stayed at the school during the week but went home to their parents on weekends. The children were presented with six cards, each presenting a story about another child's emotion-provoking experience. The participants were asked how they would feel and what they would think if such an experience happened to them. Across the vignettes, the most frequently reported emotion was sadness, reported by 42% of the children. This suggests that sadness was a familiar emotional experience for the children in the sample.

Moving House

Even if children are not physically separated from their families, they may experience sadness when their parents decide to move away from one community to another. Moving house is quite a common experience in childhood. For example, in the US, nearly 70% of children have moved from one house to another by the time they are five years old (Beck et al., 2016). Moving house is listed as a stressful life event in psychological checklists. For example, in an Australian cohort study of over 400 women and their children, the investigators found that in families who had moved more than twice in their child's first two years of life, those children had more emotional problems when they were nine years old (Rumbold et al., 2012). Their problems included anxiety as well as sadness. This association remained significant even when the investigators controlled for factors such as the child's gender, characteristics of the household, and changes in the make-up of the family.

Findings from the Millennium Cohort Study in the UK suggested that the adverse effects of moving house could be explained by some of the reasons families move, such as changing jobs and changes in the family structure (e.g., having other children or experiencing marital problems, separation, or divorce) (Gambaro & Joshi, 2016). These emotional problems may certainly include anger and fear as well as sadness.

Children's emotional problems are especially affected when they move house frequently, often changing accommodation and sometimes experiencing homelessness. In these upsetting circumstances, children may often feel angry as well as sad (Kirkman et al., 2010). Both anger and sadness might have increased when the house moves were associated with changes in the family structure, due to parents' separation and divorce.

Bereavements

Death of Pets

Approximately half of families in the UK have at least one pet (Murray et al., 2010). For many children, their first experience of grief occurs when a pet dies. Children's reactions to the death of a pet were investigated in a large longitudinal sample of children born in Bristol (Crawford et

Bereavements

Children may experience permanent separations when a beloved pet or a family member dies. These bereavements may evoke extreme sadness.

al., 2020). By the time they were eight years old, more than half the children in the sample (N = 3296) had experienced the death of a pet. On average, this occurred when the children were approaching five years of age. Those children had significantly higher scores on a questionnaire about behavioural and emotional problems than the children who had a pet that had not died (N = 1682) or those who had never had a pet (N = 808). When other factors that might influence the children's mental health were controlled for, the effect of the death of a pet was no longer statistically significant for girls; however, it still had a significant effect on boys' emotional and behavioural problems.

Death in the Family

Children's emotional reactions to the death of a family member may partly depend on their understanding of the permanence of death and the extent to which they believe in an afterlife. Their responses to a family member's death will be influenced by the beliefs and traditions of their culture.

In an essay on children's understanding of death, Paul Harris (2018) suggested that children develop an understanding of the biological facts of death while also acquiring a culturally informed view of a spiritual afterlife for the person who has died. His interviews with Spanish children whose grandparents had died discovered that most 7-year-olds were most likely to respond to questions about the grandparent's death with biological explanations, whereas for the 11-year-olds, biological and spiritual explanations were intertwined.

Bereaved children, and in particular bereaved adolescents, may respond with anger as well as grief. In a review of the literature, adolescents who have lost a parent to death have been found to feel irritable and angry, fearful, and guilty, as well as sad (Guzzo & Gobbi, 2021). In particular, many children and adolescents who have lost a parent to death suffer from depression (e.g., Stikkelbroek et al., 2012). We now turn to the topic of childhood and adolescent depression in the next chapter.

Further Reading

Arias, J. A., Williams, C., Raghvani, R., Aghajani, M., Baez, S., Belzung, C., Booij, L., Busatto, G., Chiarella, J., Fu, C. H.-Y., Ibanez, A., Liddell, B. L., Lowe, L.,

Penninx, B. W. J. H., Rosa, P., & Kemp, A. H. (2020). The neuroscience of sadness: A multidisciplinary synthesis and collaborative review. *Neuroscience and Biobehavioral Reviews, 111,* 199–228.

References

Ainsworth, M. D. S., & Bell, S. M. (1970). Attachment, exploration, and separation: Illustrated by the behaviour of one-year-olds in a strange situation. *Child Development, 41,* 49–67.

Arias, J. A., Williams, C., Raghvani, R., Aghajani, M., Baez, S., Belzung, C., Booij, L., Busatto, G., Chiarella, J., Fu, C. H.-Y., Ibanez, A., Liddell, B. L., Lowe, L., Penninx, B. W. J. H., Rosa, P., & Kemp, A. H. (2020). The neuroscience of sadness: A multidisciplinary synthesis and collaborative review. *Neuroscience and Biobehavioral Reviews, 111,* 199–228.

Beck, B., Buttaro, A., & Lennon, M. C. (2016). Home moves and child wellbeing in the first five years of life in the United States. *Longitudinal and Life Course Studies, 7,* 240–264.

Crawford, K. M., Zhu, Y., Davis, K. A., Ernst, S., Jacobsson, K., Nishimi, K., Smith, A. D. A. C., & Dunn, E. C. (2020). The mental health effect of pet death during childhood: Is it better to have loved and lost than never to have loved at all? *European Child and Adolescent Psychiatry, 30,* 1547–1558.

Duarte, T. E., Brito, B. F. L., & Reis, A. H. (2016). Parents dealing with the expression of sadness with their children. *Psico-USF, 21,* 1.

Gambaro, L., & Joshi, H. (2016). Moving home in the early years: What happens to children in the UK? *Longitudinal and Life Course Studies, 7*(3), 265–287.

Green, J. A., Whitney, P. G., & Potegal, M. (2011). Screaming, whining, yelling, and crying: Categorical and intensity differences in vocal expressions of anger and sadness in children's tantrums. *Emotion, 11,* 1124–1133.

Guzzo, M. F., & Gobbi, G. (2021). Parental death during adolescence: A review of the literature. *Omega Journal of Death and Dying, 87,* 229–244.

Harris, P. L. (2018). Children's understanding of death: From biology to religion. *Philosophical Transactions of the Royal Society B, 373*(1754), 20170267.

Izard, C. E., Fantauzzo, C., Castle, J. M., Haynes, O. M., Rayias, M. F., & Putnam, P. H. (1995). The ontogeny and significance of infants' facial expressions in the first 9 months of life. *Developmental Psychology, 31,* 997–1013.

Kingery, J. N., Peneston, K. R., Rice, S. E., & Wormuth, B. M. (2012). Parental anxious expectations and child anxiety predicting homesickness during overnight summer camp. *Journal of Outdoor Recreation, Education, and Leadership, 4*(3).

Kirkman, M., Keys, D., Bodzak, D., & Turner, A. (2010). 'Are we moving again this week?' Children's experiences of homelessness in Victoria, Australia. *Social Sciences and Medicine, 70,* 994–1001.

Lewis, M., Sullivan, M. W., & Kim, H. M.-S. (2015). Infant approach and Withdrawal in response to a goal blockage: Its antecedent causes and its effects on toddler persistence. *Developmental Psychology, 51,* 1553–1563.

Lewis, M., Sullivan, M. W., Ramsey, D. S., & Alessandri, S. M. (1992). Individual differences in anger and sad responses during extinction: Antecedents and consequences. *Infant Behavior and Development, 15,* 443–452.

Murray, J. K., Browne, W. J., Roberts, M. A., Whitmarsh, A., & Gryffydd-Jones, T. J. (2010). Number and ownership profiles of cats and dogs in the UK. *Veterinary Record, 166*, 163–169.

Oster, H., Hegley, D., & Nagel, L. (1992). Adult judgments and fine-grained analysis of infant facial expressions: Testing the validity of a priori coding formulas. *Developmental Psychology, 28*, 1115–1131.

Partridge, S. (2021). Boarding school syndrome: Reconsidered in social context and through the lens of attachment theory. *Attachment, 15*, 269–278.

Rao, Z., & Gibson, J. (2018). Motivations for emotional expression and Emotion regulation strategies in Chinese school-aged children. *Motivation and Emotion, 43*, 371–386.

Rumbold, A. R., Giles, L. C., Whitrow, M. J., Steele, E. J., Davies, C. E., Davies, M. J., & Moore, V. M. (2012). The effects of house moves during early childhood on child mental health at age 9 years. *BMC Public Health, 12*, 583.

Shiller, V. M., Izard, C. E., & Hembree, E. A. (1986). Patterns of emotion expression during separation in the strange-situation procedure. *Developmental Psychology, 22*, 378–382.

Stikkelbroek, Y., Prinzie, P., de Graaf, R., ten Have, M., & Cuijpers, P. (2012). Parental death during childhood and psychopathology in adulthood. *Psychiatry Research, 198*, 516–520.

Chapter 11

Depression in Childhood and Adolescence

Back in the 20th century, only a few psychologists and psychiatrists suggested that children might suffer from clinically defined depression (e.g., Cytryn & McKnew, 1972). Those investigators suggested that children who had suffered from a traumatic event might show symptoms of acute depression. They also suggested that children who had at least one parent with a history of depression and/or the experience of separation from their parents might suffer from chronic depression.

Other psychiatrists and psychologists at that time argued against these claims that clinicians could diagnose depression in childhood. They suggested that some of the indicators of depression, such as crying and feeling sad, were too common in childhood to be considered symptoms of a clinical disorder (e.g., Lefkowitz & Burton, 1978).

The investigators who were exploring the possibility that depression could occur in childhood faced some problems in sorting out the terminology. The word depression itself could refer to normal fluctuations in mood, indicating low spirits that all of us might experience from

Life Events

Upsetting or traumatic experiences that may trigger an episode of depression.

time to time, or a reasonable show of sadness in response to upsetting life events such as bereavements (Angold, 1988). Was that really equivalent to the depression felt by adults? Or were children's experiences of persistent sadness only precursors to the clinically defined depressive disorders of adulthood, but did not yet qualify as episodes of depressive disorders (Angold, 1993)?

However, over the next decades, studies of samples of young people in the community as well as clinical samples led to the acceptance of the idea that children could feel depressed. The acceptance of the existence of childhood depression in those children then led to attempts to use formal diagnostic criteria for a depressive disorder that could be applied to

DOI: 10.4324/9781003483793-13

Table 11.1 DSM-5 Symptoms of Depression

The presence of at least five of the following symptoms during the same two-week period accompanied by a change in functioning. At least one of the items is either a depressed mood or a loss of interest or pleasure. It is important to note that the symptoms cannot be explained by other medical conditions.

- Depressed or irritable mood most of the day, almost every day, as demonstrated by either subjective report, for example, the patient feels sad, empty, or hopeless, or observation made by others, for example, the patient appears sad.
- A significant decrease in interest or pleasure in activities most of the day, nearly every day as indicated by self-reporting or observation
- Failure to make expected weight gain or remarkable weight loss when not dieting or a remarkable weight gain, or decrease or increase in daily appetite
- Lack of sleep or excessive sleeping almost every day
- Psychomotor unrest or retardation almost every day (observable by others, not merely subjective feelings of restlessness).
- Lack of energy nearly every day
- Feelings of worthlessness or inappropriate guilt (possibly delusional) nearly every day (not merely self-reported or guilt for being sick)
- Decrease capacity to think or concentrate or indecisiveness almost every day (either by self-report or as observed by others)
- Repeated thoughts of death (not just fear of dying), recurrent suicidal ideation without specific plans, suicide attempt, or a definite plan to commit suicide

children as well as adolescents and adults. The current criteria for childhood depression in DSM-5 are presented in Table 11.1.

Features of Depression in Childhood

The investigators who have studied depression in childhood and adolescence have noted that the clearest feature of a child's or teenager's experience of depression is 'core symptoms of persistent and pervasive sadness,' which may be accompanied by feelings of guilt and low self-esteem (Maughan, Collishaw, & Stringaris, 2013). Those emotional features are sometimes associated with physical problems, including sleep difficulties and loss of appetite.

The key symptom in diagnoses of Major Depressive Disorder (MDD) is depressed mood; however, in the case of children and adolescents, either depressed mood or irritable mood would be the key feature indicating the possible diagnosis of MDD. Other core symptoms include 'diminished interest or pleasure; significant increase or reduction in weight or appetite; insomnia or hypersomnia; psychomotor agitation or retardation; loss of energy or fatigue; feelings of excessive or inappropriate guilt or worthlessness; loss of concentration, reduced ability to think, or indecisiveness; and recurrent thoughts of death; suicidal ideas; or attempts at suicide' (Thapar, Eyre, Patel, & Brent, 2022). These key symptoms reveal how young people's persistent sadness might spill out to influence other emotions and cognitions such as guilt, their motor actions, their decision-making, their self-esteem, and their persistent ideas of death and self-destruction.

Rates of Depression in Young People

As we have seen, the possibility that children might suffer from depression only began to be recognized in the last decades of the 20th century. In this century, the rates of cases of depression have been rising. In a meta-analysis of studies of the prevalence of childhood and adolescent depression over three decades from 1985 to 2012 (Polanczyk,

Prevalence

The proportion of individuals in a defined area or community who meet the diagnostic criteria for an illness, including mental illnesses such as depression.

Salum, Sugaya, Caye, & Rohde, 2015), the investigators studied the rates of children's and adolescents' depression in 47 studies that took place in 27 countries around the world. Across the different samples, 13% of the young people in the sample met the diagnostic criteria for a mental disorder. Only 2.6% met the criteria for a depressive disorder. Anxiety disorders (6.5%) and disruptive behavioural disorders (5.7%) were more prevalent.

The prevalence of child and adolescent depression increased over the following decade. In another meta-analysis of studies conducted across the world (the total number of participants across the samples being over 80,000), 25.2% of children were diagnosed with depressive and/or anxiety disorders (Racine, McArthur, Cooke, et al., 2021). This population of children was assessed during the COVID-19 pandemic. These findings draw attention to the fact that depressive disorders can reflect global events, moderated by the particular risks and positive influences in individual families. It remains to be seen if the children affected by their pandemic experiences are more vulnerable to risk factors and life events in their later years.

Gender Similarities and Differences

Beginning in the teenage years, men and boys are less likely to experience depressive illness than women and girls are. In adulthood, women are twice as likely as men to become depressed (Thapar et al, 2022). This gender gap emerges in middle childhood and increases in adolescence. For example, in a survey undertaken in England by the UK Office for National Statistics in the period right before the COVID-19 epidemic,

31% of young women between the ages of 16 and 24 years reported that they had experienced depression and/or anxiety (Office of National Statistics Reports, 2021).

In the early childhood years, depression can be identified in both girls and boys. For example, in a longitudinal study of nearly 5000 children in Australia (Lewis, Sue-Koew, Toumbourou, & Rowland, 2020), different trajectories between 4 and 15 years of age were identified. Some boys as well as girls showed signs of depression at the beginning of the study. However, girls were more likely than boys to experience an increasing level of depressive symptoms over time.

These findings raise the question of whether it is appropriate to compare adolescent girls' and boys' rates of depression at the same chronological age, given that the rate of general maturation is known to differ for girls and boys. On average, girls generally go through puberty one or two years earlier than boys do, and girls are more likely than boys to experience precocious puberty, i.e., making that transition earlier than most girls do (Fechner, 2002). However, children can experience depression prior to puberty, and both social and biological factors influence which children become depressed.

For example, in a longitudinal study of over 300 children living in a Midwestern city in the US, which began when the children were in preschool and continued for ten years (Whalen, Luby, Tilman, Mike, Barch, & Belden, 2016), the investigators identified subgroups of girls and boys who showed low, medium, and high rates of depressive symptoms. In addition to measuring the children's symptoms, the team also collected information on the children's behavioural problems, their parents' histories of depression, and the socioeconomic circumstances of their families.

The rates of depression in this sample drawn from a large city were higher than the national average. The statistical analyses identified three groups of boys and three groups of girls who showed low, medium, and high rates of depressive symptoms. Both the boys and girls in the groups that showed high rates of depressive symptoms had been most likely to have experienced social adversity and to have family members who had experienced depression. The differences between the low and medium rates of symptoms were not as strongly associated with social adversity and family histories of depression. High and medium levels of the children's depressive symptoms were also associated with the children's behavioural problems, which suggests that the family history of depression and difficult social circumstances affected children's behavioural as well as emotional problems. At this age, prior to puberty, both girls and boys were influenced by their parents' own history of depression and their family circumstances.

Continuity of Depressive Disorders from Adolescence into Adulthood

Adolescents' experience of depression in the early teenage years often predicts later vulnerability to depression in young adulthood. For example, in the longitudinal ALSPAC study of a birth cohort of children born in Bristol, England, the participants reported on their symptoms of depression and anxiety during interviews when they were 8, 10, and 13 years old. They were interviewed again when they were 24 years old (Morales-Munoz, Mallikarjun, Chandan, Thayakaram, Upthegrove, & Marwaha, 2023). At the young adult assessment, the investigators again collected information about the participants' physical and mental health. Those participants who had previously shown symptoms of anxiety, depression, or both were more likely to report physical and mental health problems at age 24. Anxiety symptoms had declined over the years while depressive symptoms had increased in the sample as a whole. Nonetheless, analyses of the longitudinal data revealed subgroups of participants who had been consistently anxious, or depressed, or both over the years from childhood to early adulthood. These findings suggest that for some individuals, depressive episodes occur more than once across childhood, adolescence, and adulthood, not just in response to specific life events. In addition, these patterns of symptoms across the years suggest that there may be links between individuals' fearfulness and sadness as they grow older. These findings remind us that children with emotional problems may meet the criteria for more than one clinical diagnosis. Their combination of symptoms from different emotional and behavioural sets of problems will require looking beyond a 'primary diagnosis.'

Further Reading

Thapar, A., Eyre, O., Patel, V., & Brent, D. (2022). Depression in young people. *Lancet, 400*, 617–631.

References

Angold, A. (1988). Childhood and adolescent depression: I. Epidemiological and aetiological aspects. *British Journal of Psychiatry, 152*, 601–617.

Angold, A. (1993). Why do we not know the cause of depression in children? In D. F. Hay & A. Angold (Eds.), *Precursors and causes in development and psychopathology.* Chichester: Wiley.

Cytryn, L., & McKnew, D. H. (1972). Proposed classification of childhood depression. *American Journal of Psychiatry, 129*, 149–155.

Fechner, P. A. (2002). Gender differences in puberty. *Journal of Adolescent Health, 305*, 44–48.

Lefkowitz, M. M., & Burton, N. (1978). Childhood depression: A critique of the concept. *Psychological Bulletin, 85,* 716–726.

Lewis, A. J., Sae-Koew, J. H., Toumbourou, J. W., & Rowland, B. (2020). Gender differences in trajectories of depressive symptoms across childhood and adolescence: A multi-group growth mixture model. *Journal of Affective Disorders, 260,* 463–472.

Maughan, B., Collishaw, S., & Stringaris, A. (2013). Depression in childhood and adolescence. *Journal of the Canadian Academy of Child and Adolescent Psychiatry, 22,* 35–40.

Morales-Munoz, I., Mallikarjun, P. K., Chandan, J. S., Thayakaram, R., Upthegrove, R., & Marwaha, S. (2023). Impact of anxiety and depression across adolescence on Adverse outcomes in young adulthood: A UK birth cohort study. *British Journal of Psychiatry, 222,* 212–220.

Office of National Statistics Reports. (2021). https://www.ons.gov.uk/peoplepo pulationandcommunity/wellbeing

Polanczyk, G. V., Salum, G. A., Sugaya, L. S., Caye, A., & Rohde, L. A. (2015). Annual research review: A meta-analysis of the worldwide prevalence of mental disorders in children and adolescents. *Journal of Child Psychology and Psychiatry, 56,* 345–365.

Racine, N., McArthur, B. A., Cooke, J. D., Eirich, R., Zhu, J., & Madigan, S. (2021). Global prevalence of depressive and anxiety symptoms in children and adolescents during COVID-19. *JAMA Pediatrics, 175,* 1142–1150.

Thapar, A., Eyre, O., Patel, V., & Brent, D. (2022). Depression in young people. *Lancet, 400,* 617–631.

Whalen, D. J, Luby, J. L., Tilman, J., Mike, A., Barch, D., & Belden, A. C. (2016). Latent class profiles of depressive symptoms from early to middle childhood: Predictors, outcomes, and gender effects. *Journal of Child Psychology and Psychiatry, 57,* 704–804.

Key Impacts on Research, Practice, and Policy

By the end of Section 3, you will have learnt about:

- The clinically focused prevention and intervention research that has influenced policy decisions.
- Several areas of research on children's emotions and emotional problems that are addressing contemporary concerns about children's physical and mental health.

DOI: 10.4324/9781003483793-14

Chapter 12

Key Topic
Impacts of Research on Children's Emotions on Practice and Policy

The research on emotional development, as described in the preceding chapters, has drawn attention to the proportion of children and teenagers who meet the criteria to be diagnosed with clinically significant emotional disorders. In this chapter, we focus on children's and adolescents' experiences with anxiety disorders, oppositional defiant disorder, conduct disorder, and major depression.

Prevalence of Children's and Adolescents' Emotional Disorders

In a systematic review of studies of European children's and teenagers' mental health problems, beginning with a set of over 4,000 potentially relevant articles, the investigators focused on 17 studies that met their inclusion criteria: population-based epidemiological studies of 5- to 18-year-olds living in European countries where the samples had been assessed using DSM or ICD criteria for measuring symptoms of mental health disorders (Sacco, Camilleri, Eberhardt, Umla-Runge, & Newbury-Birch, 2024). In total, the sample from those 17 studies included 50,605 participants from 14 different European countries. Overall, 15.5% of the sample met the diagnostic criteria for a mental health disorder, with the rates differing across countries, ranging from 5.7% in Denmark to 36.7% in Turkey.

In those analyses, the prevalence rates of particular emotional disorders differed across countries. On average, 7.9% of the children and adolescents met the criteria for anxiety disorders; 1.9% for oppositional defiant disorder; 1.5% for conduct disorder; and 1.7% for major depressive disorder. However, with respect to Major Depressive Disorder, the rates differed by age: 0.6% of primary school-aged children, compared to 2.5% of adolescents, met the diagnostic criteria. These data suggest that a significant number of children across diverse European countries are dealing with a variety of emotional problems.

DOI: 10.4324/9781003483793-15

Prevalence rates for children's and adolescents' mental health problems are likely to change, depending on circumstances affecting the population as a whole. For example, the rate of mental health problems amongst 5- to 16-year-olds in the UK increased from 11% in 2017 to 16% during the 2020 Covid-19 pandemic lockdown (Newlove-Delgado, McManus, Sadler, Thandi, Vizard, Cartright, & Ford, 2021).

The Impact of Covid-19

Unsurprisingly, children's and teenagers' emotional problems in particular rose during the Covid-19 pandemic. A meta-analysis of 19 studies was conducted (Racine, McArthur, Cooke, Eirich, Zhu, & Madigan, 2021), drawing from samples in Europe, North America, the Middle East, Central America, and South America (for a total of 80,879 participants). One in four participants (25.2%) experienced elevated symptoms of depression; one in five (20.5%) were experiencing symptoms of anxiety. These rates were compared to prevalence rates of depression and anxiety disorders prior to the pandemic, which were 12.9% for depression and 11.6% for anxiety; symptoms of those emotional disorders had doubled with the onset of the pandemic.

The findings from these studies and meta-analyses show how children's and teenagers' emotions are affected by the broader context of when and where they live. The rates of emotional problems differ across cultural contexts and are sensitive to global threats. Individual differences in children's vulnerability to emotional problems are always present and are important to study over time.

Intervention Studies

Different Approaches to Interventions on Emotional Problems

Intervention Studies

Studies that are designed to ameliorate existing emotional, behavioural, or mental health problems, often with novel programmes that help children deal with their existing problems. These studies are often longitudinal, with assessments of outcomes after the interventions.

Even before the onset of the Covid-19 pandemic, concerns were raised about the level of emotional problems in primary school-aged children. For example, in a longitudinal study of a community sample of firstborn children, parents were interviewed about their children's mental health at age seven using the Preschool Age Psychiatric Assessment (PAPA; Egger et al., 2006). Fifty percent of the children whose parents were interviewed met the DSM diagnostic criteria for an anxiety disorder; other emotional problems related to anger and sadness were also reported (Hay et al., 2021).

The rising rate of emotional problems in primary school pupils has led to a number of school-based intervention studies. Different studies focus on different dimensions of children's problems but yield information about behaviour, emotion, and adaptation to school environments.

For example, a systematic review identified a number of school-based intervention programmes that have taken place in different countries over the last few decades, targeting children's behavioural problems and mental health (Pilling et al., 2020). Some of those studies focused especially on emotional problems, including depression and anxiety. The studies are diverse, with some focusing on ways to prevent emotional problems and others on treatment of severe problems that were already present. Some of the studies measured declines in symptoms of depression and anxiety following the intervention; others focused on clinically defined disorders. It is noteworthy that many of these interventions that were being analysed had been carried out in the last century. However, some novel approaches have been taken in recent intervention studies. For example, some recent intervention studies have used computer gaming to work with young people with emotional problems.

Some research teams have used 'applied games' that are specifically designed to use computer games to assess and reduce symptoms of mental health problems (Fleming et al., 2017). For example, in a systematic review, the authors drew attention to some applied games (*Mindlight*, *Dojo*, *New Horizon*, and *gNATS Island*) that have been used to help reduce children's anxiety symptoms (Halldorsson, Hill, Waite, Partridge, Freeman, & Creswell, 2021). In some of the studies that were reviewed, the experience of playing the applied game did seem to reduce the participants' anxiety symptoms, but so did the comparison condition, playing a computer game that was not intentionally designed to reduce anxiety. In four other studies using applied games, the focus of the intervention, which used a game called SPARX, was on depressive symptoms. Depressive symptoms in the game-playing group were somewhat reduced in comparison with a waiting list control group.

Prevention Studies

Intervention studies are designed to reduce children's psychological problems that need to be dealt with as soon as possible. In contrast, prevention studies are experiments that usually draw upon current psychological theory; they attempt to foster positive outcomes.

Prevention Studies

Studies that draw on the existing literature to identify and test factors that might prevent emotional, behavioural, or mental health problems. These studies are typically longitudinal, with assessments of outcomes following the prevention programme.

The World Health Organization (WHO) has defined different approaches for preventing ill health, including mental health. In the context of mental health, the term 'primary prevention' refers to attempts to prevent the onset of a disease or a disorder, whereas 'secondary prevention' refers to attempts to lower the rate of people who succumb to that disease or disorder; 'tertiary prevention' refers to the methods used to reduce the physical and psychological problems caused by the disease or disorder (Fusar-Poli et al., 2021).

In the context of children's emotional development, prevention methods would involve observations and assessments of children's behaviour in early to middle childhood. The emotion theorist Carroll Izard has argued for theory-led prevention studies that would focus on emotional development. He noted that emotions make a fundamental contribution to humans' adaptation to their environments, underlying people's abilities to form social relationships, solve problems, and pursue communal as well as individual goals. He pointed out that our emotions interact with our cognitive skills in a reciprocal way. Thus, he argued that prevention programmes designed to promote cognitive or social skills must not forget to consider the children's emotions (Izard, Fantauzzo, Castle, Haynes, Reylas, & Putnam, 1995).

Prevention programmes have been designed to lower the odds that children will suffer from emotional disorders, in particular anxiety and depression. Some prevention research is carried out in samples that are representative of the general population. Other prevention studies focus on those children who are most at risk of developing emotional disorders, due to family risk factors (e.g., parents' history of emotional disorders), the environments in which they are growing up, and the life events they may have experienced.

Prevention of Anxiety Disorders

In 2019, prior to the Covid-19 pandemic, scientists had estimated that 117 million children and adolescents around the world were affected by anxiety disorders (Hugh-Jones, Becket, Tumelty, & Mallikarjun, 2019). Prevention studies are necessary to understand how these rates can be reduced. Some studies that aim to prevent children's anxiety disorders recruit samples from the general population, e.g., children in school classrooms who may or may not have shown signs of worry and anxiety.

However, children whose mothers have experienced anxiety disorders are at heightened risk for anxiety disorders themselves, so some investigators have focused on such children at higher risk for severe outcomes (Lawrence, Rooke, & Creswell, 2017). For example, the children of mothers who had themselves experienced separation anxiety disorder (SAD) prior to their children's birth were more likely to show high levels of separation anxiety symptoms as they approached their sixth birthdays (Lawrence, Cresswell, Cooper, & Murray, 2020). It is likely that targeted prevention programmes might be more effective, but identifying children in classrooms who are most at risk for anxiety disorders would be difficult and would raise ethical issues.

Prevention of Oppositional Defiant Disorder (ODD)

Prevention programmes that target ODD may use general samples of young children who might or might not go on to develop ODD. Alternatively, they may focus specifically on a subgroup of young children who are already showing early, subclinical signs of anger, oppositional behaviour, and defiance (Hawes, Gardner, Dadds, Frick, Kimonis, Burke, & Fairchild, 2023).

Many of these programmes, especially those that focus on early childhood, include parents, helping parents to respond to their children's oppositional behaviour in more constructive ways. One aim of such programmes is to foster the parents' warmth and pleasant interactions with their children as well as constructive conflict. Child-focused programmes that encourage the development of social problem-solving skills and may include elements of cognitive behaviour therapy are more useful with older children.

Prevention of Adolescent Depression

UK economists have noted that prevention strategies to tackle adolescent depression are necessary, not just for the health and well-being of depressed young people, but also for the national economy as a whole (McDaid, Park, & Wahlbeck, 2019; McDaid, Park, Davidson, Knifton, McDaid, Morton, Thorpe, & Wilson, 2022). These economists proposed that national support for anti-bullying programmes, brief psychological interventions, 'Mental Health First Aid,' exercise promotion, and programmes that facilitate 'transitions to adult life' would reduce the rates of depression and anxiety in young people. They note, however, that while some of these programmes have been found to be successful and economically feasible in other countries, they have not all been effective in the UK. It should also be noted that much of the policy-related research cited has taken place in England; health policies will differ somewhat across the four devolved nations of the UK.

Promoting Happiness

The intervention and prevention studies just discussed are accompanied by a line of intervention research that seeks to promote children's positive emotional well-being, not just reduce their sad, angry, and anxious feelings. For example, in a systematic review of published intervention studies undertaken in schools between 2000 and 2016, five studies of primary school pupils and seven studies of secondary school pupils were examined for positive signs of the children's well-being as well as their symptoms of anxiety and depression. The studies differed in several ways, including procedures and choice of outcome variables. There were some positive outcomes for the primary school pupils, but the effect sizes were small and there was little evidence for positive outcomes in the secondary school sample. It will be important to develop a broader battery of measures of positive behaviours as well as cognitive outcomes in prevention and intervention studies if we are to understand how children's positive emotions can thrive in their school settings. Reduction of negative emotions is an insufficient measure of children's well-being.

Further Reading

Cooper, K., Hards, E., Moltrecht, B., Reynolds, S., Shum, A., McElroy, E., & Loades, M. (2021). Loneliness, social relationships, and mental health in adolescents during the COVID-19 pandemic. *Journal of Affective Disorders*, *289*, 98–104.

References

Egger, H. L., Erkanli, A., Keeler, G., Potts, E., Walter, B. K., & Angold, A. (2006). Test-retest reliability of the Preschool Age Psychiatric Assessment (PAPA). *Journal of the American Academy of Child and Adolescent Psychiatry*, *45*, 538–549.

Fleming, T., Bavin, L., Stasiak, K., Hermansson-Webb, E., Merry, S. N., Cheek, C., Lucassen, M., Lau, H. M., Pollmuller, B., & Hetrick, S. (2017). Serious games and gamification for mental health: Current status and promising directions. *Frontiers in Psychiatry*, *7*, 215.

Fusar-Poli, P., Correll, C. U., Arango, C., Berk, M., Patel, V., & Ioannidis, J. P. A. (2021). Preventive psychiatry: A blueprint for improving the mental health of young people. *World Psychiatry*, *20*, 200–221.

Halldorsson, B., Hill, C., Waite, P., Partridge, K., Freeman, D., & Creswell, C. (2021). Annual research review: Immersive virtual reality and digital applied gaming interventions for the treatment of mental health problems: The need for rigorous treatment development and clinical evaluation. *Journal of Child Psychology and Psychiatry*, *62*, 584–605.

Hawes, D. J., Gardner, F., Dadds, M. R., Frick, P. J., Kimonis, E. R., Burke, J. D., & Fairchild, G. (2023). Oppositional defiant disorder. *Nature Reviews*, *9*, Article No. 31.

Hay, D. F., Paine, A. L., Perra, O., Cook, K. V., Hashmi, S., Robinson, C., Kairis, V., & Slade, R. (2021). Prosocial and aggressive behaviour: A longitudinal study. *Monographs of the Society for Research in Child Development, 86*, Serial No. 341.

Hugh-Jones, S., Becket, S., Tumelty, E., & Mallikarjun, P. (2021). Indicated prevention Interventions for anxiety in children and adolescents: A review and Meta-analysis of school-based programs. *European Child and Adolescent Psychiatry, 30*, 849–860.

Izard, C. E., Fantauzzo, C., Castle, J. M., Haynes, O. M., Rayias, M. F., & Putnam, P. H. (1995). The ontogeny and significance of infants' facial expressions in the first 9 months of life. *Developmental Psychology, 31*, 997–1013.

Lawrence, P. J., Cresswell, C., Cooper, P. J., & Murray, L. (2020). The role of maternal anxiety subtype, parenting, and infant stable temperament inhibition in child anxiety: A prospective longitudinal study. *Journal of Child Psychology and Psychiatry, 61*, 779–788.

Lawrence, P. J., Rooke, S. M., & Creswell, C. (2017). Review: Prevention of anxiety among at-risk children and adolescents—a systematic review and meta-analysis. *Child and Adolescent Mental Health, 22*, 118–130.

McDaid, D., Park, A.-L., Davidson, G., John, A., Knifton, L., McDaid, S., Morton, A., Thorpe, L., & Wilson, N. (2022). *The economic case for investing in the prevention of mental health conditions in the UK.* Commissioned Report by the Mental Health Foundation.

McDaid, D., Park, A.-L., & Wahlbeck, K. (2019). The economic case for the prevention of mental illness. *Annual Review of Public Health, 40*, 8.1–8.17.

Newlove-Delgado, T., McManus, S., Sadler, K., Thandi, S., Vizard, T., Cartright, C., & Ford, T. (2021). Child mental health in England before and during the COVID-19 lockdown. *Lancet Psychiatry, 8*, 353–354.

Pilling, S., Fonagy, P., Allison, E., Barnett, P., Campbell, C., Constantinou, M., Gardner, T., Lorenzini, N., Matthews, H., Ryan, A., Sacchetti, S., Truscott, A., Ventura, T., Watchorn, K., Whittington, C., & Kendall, T. (2020). Long-term outcomes of psychological interventions on children's and young people's Mental health: A systematic review and meta-analysis. *PLoS One, 15*, e0236525

Racine, N., McArthur, B. A., Cooke, J. D., Eirich, R., Zhu, J., & Madigan, S. (2021). Global prevalence of depressive and anxiety symptoms in children and Adolescents during COVID-19. *JAMA Pediatrics, 175*, 1142–1150.

Sacco, R., Camilleri, N., Eberhardt, J., Umla-Runge, K., & Newbury-Birch, D. (2024). A systematic review and meta-analysis of the prevalence of mental disorders Among children and adolescents in Europe. *European Child and Adolescent Psychiatry, 33*, 2877–2894.

Key Emerging Areas

By the end of Section 4, you will have learnt about several new areas of research on young people's emotional reactions to many different personal, social, and global problems, including:

- The recent increases in the rates of young people's mental health problems
- The rise in loneliness
- Adolescents' concerns about body image
- Gender dysphoria
- Racism and prejudice
- War and political unrest
- Climate change and natural disasters

DOI: 10.4324/9781003483793-16

Chapter 13

Key Topic

Emerging Areas of Novel Research on Children's Emotional Development

In the last few years, children's and adolescents' emotional development has been directly impacted by global events over which neither young people nor adults have complete control. These events include the Covid-19 pandemic but also exposure to other diseases, regional wars, political upheavals, economic distress, and changing cultural norms about what the future holds for young people. These multiple factors have a direct impact on families' social and economic needs but also on children's and adolescents' possible futures. In this final chapter, we shall consider some of the recently published research that focuses on young people's personal and political feelings in the face of global threats and sociopolitical change. First, however, we will examine some of the factors that are associated with a rise in young people's mental health problems with a particular focus on emotional disorders.

The Rise in Young People's Mental Health Problems in the UK

In a recent analysis of two large data sets of anonymized general practice records from the General Practice Research Datalink (Cybulski, Ashcroft, Carr, Garg, Chew-Graham, Kapur, & Webb, 2021), the investigators examined data from 9,133,246 GP patients between the ages of 1 and 20 years in the years between 2003 and 2018. They focused on anxiety disorders, ADHD, autism, depression,

Medical Records

Studies of children and adolescents with mental health problems will sometimes identify samples of individuals with those problems (and often a comparison sample without them), drawing on the records in hospitals and GP practices.

DOI: 10.4324/9781003483793-17

Diagnostic Criteria

Definitions of symptom patterns for physical and mental health problems, used in analysing interviews such as the DSM or ICD instruments for measuring mental health disorders.

and eating disorders. With respect to emotional disorders, the rates of anxiety and depression increased over the years in all age groups. The largest increases were shown by adolescents, but the rates of these disorders increased in younger children as well.

Increased rates of anxiety and depression may be due to a number of factors. Even if young people do not meet the clinical diagnostic criteria for these emotional disorders, they may struggle with persistently negative emotions about themselves, their families, and the situations that they are in.

Adolescents' Negative Feelings about Themselves

Loneliness

Loneliness is a common feeling that was recently exacerbated by the Covid-19 pandemic when in many countries families and households were required to isolate themselves from other members of their communities. Many young people who were experiencing isolation during the pandemic reported that they felt lonely. However, even before that global emergency, feelings of loneliness affected many children and teenagers.

Some psychologists have suggested that there are two types of loneliness (e.g., Salo, Juntilla, & Vourus, 2020): *social loneliness* (people's longing for their social networks) and *emotional loneliness* (a person's longing for an intimate emotional attachment). Loneliness is a psychological experience that appears to run in families. There is some evidence that loneliness is heritable; lonely children may often have lonely parents.

For example, these family patterns were explored in a longitudinal study of 318 Finnish schoolchildren who rated their degree of loneliness five times over a 2.5-year period. Items such as 'I feel isolated from others' were deemed to measure general social loneliness, whereas other items such as 'No one really knows me well' measured emotional loneliness. The children's parents also rated their own loneliness. Some gender differences were found, with the boys and fathers more likely to report emotional loneliness than the daughters and mothers. There were no significant gender differences in the measure of social loneliness. The children's reports of loneliness tended to be stable over time. Daughters' loneliness reflected their mothers' degree of loneliness; the same positive correlation was found for sons and their fathers. These findings suggest that families as a whole may feel disconnected from their communities, and a sense of isolation from other people may transfer from one generation to the next.

Body Image

As children grow older and their bodies change as they undergo puberty, their feelings about their bodies are likely to change as well. Many individuals find the transition to adolescence complicated and difficult; some find that they now have quite negative feelings about their changed bodies. Much attention has been paid to adolescent girls' negative feelings about their bodies, but adolescent boys are also concerned about their body images.

To examine the development of body image over the transition from childhood to adolescence, a longitudinal study of British adolescents (328 girls and 429 boys) was carried out (Lacroix, Atkinson, Garbett, & Diedrichs, 2020). The teenagers in the sample were enrolled in two coeducational secondary schools in the south of England, one whose population was more economically advantaged and the other less so, as indicated by the number of free school meals provided to pupils in both schools. The participants completed questionnaires that measured their feelings about their bodies; their views about ideal physical appearances; whether or not they felt pressured to change their appearances, for example by losing weight or bodybuilding; how they compared their appearance to other teenagers they knew and to media personalities; whether or not they had ever been teased about their appearances by other people; and whether or not they dieted to reduce their weight. The adolescents were also asked about their general self-esteem and whether they felt generally positive or had negative feelings about themselves.

Not all individuals follow the same pathways through their teenage years. The investigators used longitudinal statistical models to identify subgroups in the sample who showed different patterns of feelings about their body image over time, beginning in Year 7 when they were 11 years old on average and ending in Year 11 when they were 15. One subgroup (39% of the full sample) had highly positive feelings about their bodies at age 11, which increased slightly over the next two years and then returned to the baseline level of positive bodily esteem. Two-thirds of that very positive subgroup were boys.

Another subgroup (46% of the full sample) had moderate self-esteem about their bodies at age 11, but their levels of bodily self-esteem decreased over the years of secondary school (from Year 7 to Year 10) and then increased slightly in Year 11. The participants' final subgroup, with more negative feelings about their bodies that were consistent over time, were primarily girls (girls making up 82% of that subgroup).

Girls' higher rates of negative feelings about their bodies have been attributed to current sociocultural pressures on adolescent girls, including the high levels of using social media and some evidence that girls and boys experience social media differently (e.g., Choukas-Bradley, Roberts, Maheux, & Nesi, 2022). One feature that adolescents experience with their current social media is the proliferation of photos of friends, acquaintances, and unknown celebrities, all of whom call out for social comparison with oneself. Adolescent girls' preoccupation with their physical appearance, compared to others, has been linked to increasing rates of depression and eating disorders (Choukas-Bradley, et al., 2022). More research on the pre-adolescent risk factors for these increasingly common problems with body image might clarify the effect of past experiences that make some adolescents more vulnerable to the messages they are processing from social media.

Gender Dysphoria

Some young people are not just struggling with these gender-related issues of body image; they do not feel positive about the gender identities that were assigned at the time of their births and seek medically provided gender change.

The concept of gender identity refers to a person's self-identification as male, female, both, or neither. When a person's gender identity does not line up with the gender that person was assigned at birth, that person may have strong feelings of gender dysphoria.

Gender dysphoria has been defined as a mental health problem in the current edition of the Diagnostic and Statistical Manual, DSM-5 (see Thompson, Sarovic, Wilson, Samfjord, & Gillberg, 2022). In the context of the DSM diagnostic system, gender dysphoria is discussed as feelings that result from a contradiction between a person's chromosomes and physical genitals and that person's psychological identity. In DSM-5, gender dysphoria is explicitly defined as a difference between one's experienced and assigned gender, and significant distress or problems in functioning lasting for at least six months.

In past years, treatments had been used to 'cure' an individual's gender dysphoria. Those treatments are now considered to be unethical. It is now more common in some countries for children who experience gender dysphoria and their parents to be offered psychological support and counselling about possible medical approaches to take in the future (Claahsen-van der Grinten, Verhaak, Steensma, Middelberg, Roeffen, & Klink, 2022). However, psychological and medical care for children experiencing gender dysphoria remains a political issue in some political and clinical contexts.

Global Fears, Stress, and Trauma

The preceding discussion of young people's concerns with their own body images and gender identity may seem to suggest that they focus primarily on themselves and their own identities, not on other people. However, adolescence is also a time when individuals begin to focus on their feelings about the broader world and make ethical and political choices. Whether they take liberal or conservative positions on national and global issues, many adolescents become engaged in political debates and issues. Here are a few examples of young people's emotional reactions to events happening in the world and, in particular, in the UK.

Economic Hardship

A number of children and adolescents in the UK live under conditions of hardship. For example, in the longitudinal Millennium Cohort Study, which recruited the families of children who were born between 2000 and 2002, the participating families ($N = 11,726$) were assessed when the focal child had reached age 14. At that point, more than a third of families (34.5%) were living in poverty (Adjei, Schluter, Straatman, Melis, Fleming, McGovern, Howard, Kaner, Wolfe, & Taylor-Robinson, 2022). Sustained poverty was associated with other problems, such as parents' substance use and poor mental health.

Racism and Prejudice

Young people around the world face prejudice directed toward their racial and ethnic identities. This is especially true for children and adolescents from immigrant families who have sought refuge in a new country, escaping from dire conditions in their homelands. In many cases, these refugee families are not welcomed in their new countries.

For example, in a systematic review of immigrant children and adolescents' experiences of discrimination and what the authors referred to as 'everyday racism' (Metzner, Adedeji, Wichmann, Zaheer, Schneider, Schlachzig, Richters, Heumann, & Mays, 2022), the analyses revealed an impact of discrimination and racism on mental health. In some samples in the dataset, a proportion of children experienced PTSD symptoms and behavioural problems. Immigrant children were also likely to have experienced bullying (Sapouna, Amicis, & Vezzali, 2023). The young people who had experienced discrimination and racist reactions were more likely to have depressive symptoms, which may have been exacerbated by their experiences of bullying and overt prejudice. In some cases, young people were bullied for speaking their own languages.

Bullying and being bullied sometimes take place against the background of societal change and politically associated acts of violence. In some cases, political allegiances and cultural beliefs may foster bullying, which may, in turn, lead to some aggressive reprisals. For example, in a survey given to adolescents in a state-funded secondary school in the US Midwest, 212 young people answered questions about their political beliefs and values, particularly with respect to authoritarianism; their experiences of being bullied or cyberbullied, and their own engagement in bullying or cyberbullying in the last month (Donnelly, Lannin, Kanter, Parris, and Su-Russell, 2023). The pupils also completed a questionnaire on moral disengagement, which measured tendencies to blame victims and downplay the humanity of victims (Bandura, 1999). The observed link between authoritarian world views and engaging in bullying other people appeared to be mediated by the adolescents' levels of moral disengagement. The bullying was also correlated with seeing themselves as victimized by others.

War

Families make the decision to migrate from their home countries to other lands for many different reasons. One of the main reasons is to flee from war zones. Children in areas where fighting has broken out may be fleeing for their lives, often with family members who are also at risk of being killed or wounded. Even if they manage to reach safe places away from battlefields, they carry their memories of trauma and displacement; many of them will experience the symptoms of post-traumatic stress disorder (Yule, Dyregrov, Raundalen, & Smith, 2013). In a resolution of the UN Securiity Counciil, the members declared that violence against children in the context of war is a violation of children's human rights.

Children exposed to war have a higher rate of stress and other emotional disorders; they experience fears and anxiety, especially if they experience separation from their family members (Burgin et al., 2022). If they have managed to escape actual battlefields, they may then spend long periods of time in refugee camps before they are able to settle in new, safer communities. These refugee experiences may also be distressing and may, in themselves, induce more trauma. If they reach safe havens away from wartime violence, refugee children are not always welcomed by their new communities. They may still be grieving the loss of family and friends, and not yet able to acquire all the language skills and customs needed to adapt to their new circumstances.

Climate Change and Natural Disasters

Children may also experience displacement due to the effects of climate change. Experiences of the impacts of global warming, such as higher temperatures and rising sea levels, have adverse effects on children's and adolescents' emotional well-being (e.g., Clemens, von Hirschhausen, & Fegert, 2022). These effects are both direct (when families' homes and communities are destroyed by fire or flooding) and indirect, when climate effects may lead to food insecurity. Because climate change is likely to have even more adverse effects in the future, children and adolescents may experience high degrees of climate-related anxiety and depression (Clemens et al., 2022). Some investigators refer specifically to young people's *eco-anxiety* (e.g., Leger-Goodes, Malboeuf-Hurtubuise, Mastine, Genereux, Paradis, & Camden, 2022). For example, in those authors' scoping review of studies of children's feelings about climate change published since 2002, the most commonly used words by the participants were *worry* and *hope*. These two emotion words were positively correlated. These findings suggest that children are aware of dire possibilities for climate disasters, but that awareness goes along with their cautious optimism about the prospects for the future.

Further Reading

Clemens, V., von Hirschhausen, E., & Fegert, J.M. (2022). Report of the Intergovernmental Panel on Climate Change: Implications for the mental health policy of children and adolescents in Europe—a scoping review. *European Child and Adolescent Psychiatry, 31*, 701–713.

Firth, J., Solmi, N., Löchner, J., Cortese, S., Lopéz-Gil, J.F., Machaczek, K., Lambert, J., Fabian, H., Fabiano, N., & Torous, J. (2025). Promoting healthy digital device usage: Recommendations for youth and parents. *World Psychiatry, 24*, 1–2.

Lacroix, E., Atkinson, M. J., Garbett, K. M., & Diedrichs, P. C. (2020). One size does not fit all: Trajectories of body image development and their predictors in early adolescence. *Development and Psychopathology, 34*, 285–294.

McGorry, P. D., Mei, C., Dalal, N., Alvarez-Jimenez, M., Blakemore, S.-J., Browne, V., et al. (2024). The *Lancet* Commission on Youth Mental Health. *The Lancet Psychiatry Commissions, 11*, 731–774.

Metzner, F., Adedeji, A., Wichmann, M. L.-Y., Zaheer, Z., Schneider, L., Schlachzig, L., Richters, J., Heumann, S., & Mays, D. (2022). Experiences of discrimination and everyday racism among children and adolescents with an immigrant background: Results of a systematic literature review on the impact of discrimination on the developmental outcomes of minors worldwide. *Frontiers in Psychology: Developmental Psychology, 13*, 977949.

References

Adjei, N. K., Schluter, D. K., Straatman, V. S., Melis, G., Fleming, K. M., McGovern, R., Howard, L. M., Kaner, E., Wolfe, I., & Taylor-Robinson, D. C. (2022). Impact of poverty and family adversity on adolescent health: A multi-trajectory analysis using the UK Millennium Cohort Study. *The Lancet Regional Health Europe, 13*, 100279.

Bandura, A. (1999). Selective moral disengagement in the exercise of moral agency. *Personalality and Social Psychology Review, 3*, 101–119.

Burgin, D., Anagnostopoulus, D., The Board and Policy Division of ESCAP, Vitiello, B., Sukale, T., Schmid, M., & Fegert, J.M. (2022). Impact of war and forced displacement on children's mental health: Multilevel, needs-oriented, and trauma-Informed approaches. *European Child and Adolescent Psychiatry, 31*, 845–853.

Choukas-Bradley, S., Roberts, S. R., Maheux, A. J., & Nesi, J. (2022). The perfect storm: A developmental-sociocultural framework for the role of social media in adolescent girls' body image concerns and mental health. *Clinical Child and Family Psychology Review, 25*, 681–701.

Claahsen-van der Grinten, H., Verhaak, C., Steensma, T., Middelberg, T., Roeffen, J., & Klink, D. (2022). Gender incongruence and gender dysphoria in childhood and adolescence: Current insights in diagnostics, management, and follow-up. *European Journal of Pediatrics, 180*, 1349–1357.

Clemens, V., von Hirschhausen, E., & Fegert, J. M. (2022). Report of the Intergovernmental panel on climate change: Implications for the mental health policy of children and adolescents in Europe—a scoping review. *European Child and Adolescent Psychiatry, 31*, 701–713.

Cybulski, L., Ashcroft, D. M., Carr, M. J., Shruti Garg, C., Chew-Graham, A., Kapur, N., & Webb, R. T. (2021). Temporal trends in annual incidence rates for psychiatric disorders and self-harm among children and adolescents in the UK, 2003–2018. *BMC Psychiatry, 21*, Article number 229.

Donnelly, M. E., Lannin, D. G., Kanter, G. B., Parris, L., & Su-Russell, C. (2023). The social-cognitive attitudes of teen bullies: Right-wing authoritarianism, moral disengagement, and perceived victimization. *International Journal of Bullying Prevention*, published online.

Lacroix, E., Atkinson, M. J., Garbett, K. M., & Diedrichs, P. C. (2020). One size does not fit all: Trajectories of body image development and their predictors in early adolescence. *Development and Psychopathology, 34*, 285–294.

Leger-Goodes, T., Malboeuf-Hurtubise, C., Mastine, T., Genereux, M., Paradis, P.-O., & Camden, C. (2022). Eco-anxiety in children: A scoping review of the mental health impacts of the awareness of climate change. *Current Trends in Environmental Psychology, 4*, 100182.

Metzner, F., Adedeji, A., Wichmann, M. L-Y., Zaheer, Z., Schneider, L., Schlachzig, L., Richters, J., Heumann, S., & Mays, D. (2022). Experiences of discrimination and everyday racism among children and adolescents with an immigrant background: Results of a systematic literature review on the impact of discrimination on the developmental outcomes of minors worldwide. *Frontiers in Psychology: Developmental Psychology, 13*, 977949.

Salo, A.-E., Junttilla, N., & Vauras, M. (2020). Parental self-efficacy and intra- and extra-Familial relationships. *Journal of Child and Family Studies, 31*, 2714–2729.

Sapouna, M., de Amicis, L., & Vezzali, L. (2023). Bullying victimization due to racial, ethnic, citizenship, and/or religious status: A systematic review. *Adolescent Research Review, 8*, 261–296.

Thompson, L., Sarovic, D., Wilson, P., Samfjord, A., & Gillberg, C. (2022). A PRISMA systematic review of adolescent gender dysphoria literature: (2) mental health. *PLOS Global Public Health*, *2*(5), e0000426.

Yule, W., Dyregrov, A., Raundalen, M., & Smith, P. (2013). Children and war: The work of the Children and War Foundation. *European Journal of Psychotraumatology*, *4*, 1–7.

Index

Page numbers in **bold** indicate tables

For Product Safety Concerns and Information please contact our EU
representative GPSR@taylorandfrancis.com
Taylor & Francis Verlag GmbH, Kaufingerstraße 24, 80331 München, Germany

www.ingramcontent.com/pod-product-compliance
Lightning Source LLC
Chambersburg PA
CBHW070347270326
41926CB00017B/4032